Sun Tzu's THE ART OF WAR

孫子兵法

Plus The Art of Love

Winning Romantic Battles

Gary Gagliardi

"A Pleasure to Read"

"I found this book a pleasure to read. I have always been intrigued by the fact that many ancient teachings of the orient can still be applied to everyday life even now...*The Art of War Plus The Art of Love* is enthusiastically recommended to anyone seeking to improve their social and personal communication skills (especially with respect to decision making matters relevant to romance and courtship), as a particularly insightful blending of interpretation of ancient wisdom with contemporary realities."

January 2002, *Midwest Book Review*, JAMES A. COX
Editor-in-Chief

This book contains the only award-winning translation of Sun Tzu's *The Art of War*

*The Art of War Plus
The Ancient Chinese Revealed*

Multicultural Nonfiction
Independent Publishers
Book Award
2003 - Winner

Award Recognition for *Art of War* Strategy Books by Gary Gagliardi

The Golden Key to Strategy

Psychology/Self-Help
Ben Franklin
Book Award
2006 - Winner

The Art of War Plus The Ancient Chinese Revealed

Multicultural Nonfiction
Independent Publishers
Book Award
2003 - Winner

Making Money by Speaking: The Spokesperson Strategy

Career
Foreword Magazine
Book of the Year
2007 - Finalist

Strategy for Sales Managers

Business
Independent Publishers
Book Award
2006 - Semi-Finalist

The Warrior Class: 306 Lessons in Strategy

Self-Help
Foreword Magazine
Book of the Year
2005 - Finalist

Strategy Against Terror

Philosophy
Foreword Magazine
Book of the Year
2005 - Finalist

The Ancient Bing-fa: Martial Arts Strategy

Sports
Foreword Magazine
Book of the Year
2007 - Finalist

The Art of War Plus Its Amazing Secrets

Multicultural Nonfiction
Independent Publishers
Book Award
2005 - Finalist

The Warrior's Apprentice

Youth Nonfiction
Independent Publishers
Book Award
2006 - Semi-Finalist

Published by
Science of Strategy Institute, Clearbridge Publishing
  suntzus.com   scienceofstrategy.org

Third Edition
ISBN 978-1-929194-49-0(13-digit) 1-929194-49-8 (10-digit)
Also titled in a previous edition: *The Art of War for The Management Warrior*
Copyright 1999, 2000, 2001, 2003, 2004, 2007, 2014 Gary Gagliardi
Registered with Department of Copyrights, Library of Congress
Registration Number TX 5-757-034

All rights reserved. No part of this book may be reproduced or transmitted in any part or by any means, electronic or mechanical, including photocopying, recording, or by any information storage and retrieval system, without the written permission of the Publisher, except where permitted by law.

Interior and cover graphic design by Dana and Jeff Wincapaw.
Original Chinese calligraphy by Tsai Yung, Green Dragon Arts, www.greendragonarts.com.

Publisher's Cataloging-in-Publication Data
Sun-tzu, 6th cent. B.C.
  [Sun-tzu ping fa, English]
  The art of war plus the art of love Sun Tzu and Gary Gagliardi.
  p. 222 cm. 23
  Includes introduction to basic competitive philosophy of Sun Tzu
    1. Family and Relationships—Love and Romance—U.S.
    2..Military art and science - Early works to 1800.
    I. Gagliardi, Gary 1951— . II. The Art of War Plus The Art of love
HD31.S764413 2000
658.8 /4 21 —dc19
                    Library of Congress Control Number: 2002090339

Science of Strategy Institute/Clearbridge Publishing
2829 Linkview Dr. Las Vegas, NV, 89134
Phone: (702) 721-9631
garyg@suntzus.com
scienceofstrategy.org

Sun Tzu's
THE ART OF WAR

Plus
The Art of Love

Winning Romantic Battles

by Gary Gagliardi

Science of Strategy Institute
Clearbridge Publishing

Contents

The Art of War Plus
The Art of Love

	Foreword: Using Romantic Strategy............ 8
	Introduction: Sun Tzu's Strategic System. 16
1	Analysis 23
	Finding Love 25
2	Going to War... 37
	Rewarding Relationships 39
3	Planning an Attack.................................... 49
	Looking for Love 51
4	Positioning.. 61
	Getting Closer.................................... 63
5	Momentum 73
	Intense Intimacy 75
6	Weakness and Strength 85
	Needs and Satisfaction..................... 87
7	Armed Conflict 101
	Relationship Friction.......................103
8	Adaptability 115
	Personal Flexibility.......................... 117
9	Armed March..125
	Love's Path 127
10	Field Position 145
	Warning Signs..................................147
11	Types of Terrain 163
	Relationship Stages......................... 165
12	Attacking with Fire 189
	Heart's Desire................................... 191
13	Using Spies 201
	Knowing Another............................203
	Glossary of Key Strategic Concepts 214
	Index of Topics in *The Art of War* 220

Foreword

Using Romantic Strategy

Over the years, this work has drawn vehement criticism. Fortunately, this criticism has not from those who have read it. Readers generally find it both useful and interesting. This criticism comes from those who do not like the concept of such a book, marrying war and love. As you might suspect, these critics fall into two, very different philosophical categories.

One group looks down upon romance. They think that this work "cheapens" the principles of Sun Tzu. Romance is too trivial to be considered a "serious" form of competition. They think Sun Tzu's ideas are too important to apply to something as frivolous as the pursuit of love. War and other forms of serious competition are should not be brought down to the emotional level of winning affection.

Just as vehemently, the second group looks down upon the idea of war. They are horrified at the thought that the same principles that create success on the battlefield might also be used to create success in relationships. In their minds, war is evil and love is holy. We should "make love, not war." Sun Tzu, in writing a book on military success is by evil almost by definition. His ideas , therefore, must be shunned and never applied to something as sacred as personal relationships.

In my view, both of these groups are mistaken both about Sun Tzu and the nature of relationships.

Both groups, and many others as well, are confused about the nature of competition and, therefore, about the nature of Sun Tzu's work. This is especially true concerning competition that takes place in the world of relationships. This confusion arises from two false dichotomies.

The first false dichotomy is between competition and cooperation. People mistakenly think that, since cooperation means working together, competition must mean working against others. In applying the principles of competition to romance, we are escalating the battle of the sexes.

The second false dichotomy is between competition and production. People are taught to think that since cooperation is productive, competition must be destructive. By this thinking, if we want our relationships to be productive, we cannot act competitively.

Both of these viewpoints make a fundamental mistake. They confuse competition with conflict. Competitive strategy, as defined by Sun Tzu, avoids conflict. Conflict only arises from failed competitive strategies, not successful ones. Sun Tzu viewed competition from a perspective that makes it essential to both cooperation and production.

In Sun Tzu's view, competition exists everywhere there is a choice. His strategy is to make comparisons among alternative choices. Real competition takes place in the human mind. All alternatives choices are "at war" with each other within the human mind. To put it more nicely, the alternatives we can choose are in competition with each other for our decisions. Cooperation requires competition because we must choose our partners. Production requires competition because we must choose what to produce, and how to produce it.

From this perspective, it is easier to see how these ideas apply these to romance. We must make choices in our romantic life. We must choose who to pursued and how to pursue them. Those in

Foreword: Using Romantic Strategy

whom we are romantically interested must choose to encourage us or discourage our interest.

The point of Sun Tzu's work is that most people don't understand how good choices are made. There are many more categories of bad choices than there are good ones. Making good choices requires a special set of skills. Encouraging others to make the choices that we desire also requires a special set of skills. Good competitive decisions are not made in the same way that good planning or management decisions are made. Our romantic lives are not "managed" in the sense that they are in our total control. While planning depends on prioritization and organization, competitive decisions depend on agility and positioning, moving quickly and decisively though a shifting kaleidoscope of options.

Sun Tzu taught that in the realm of competitive choices, success is not a matter of winning fights with other people. Instead success depends on building and advancing strategic positions. A "position" is defined by Sun Tzu as what people actually compare in making choices. The basis of conflict in competition is trying to weaken opposing positions. In other words, romantic success does not come from discrediting our romantic rivals. Sun Tzu's taught that conflict is inherently destructive, weaken the positions of everyone involved. In attacking romantic rivals, we damage our own position as well as theirs.

The focus of Sun Tzu's system is to create positions that others do not want to challenge and that ideally they want to support. Sun Tzu teaches that a general who fights a hundred battles and wins a hundred battles is not a good general. A good general is one who finds a way to win without fighting a single battle. His strategy teaches that we win by building the right positions and advancing those positions while avoiding conflict.

Love is a battle. Success is not an accident. Sun Tzu's strategy works because romance, whether we realize it our not, is a competition, a comparison of options. We win the best possible romantic partner in a complex contest. This contest is as old as the biology of sex and it hasn't grown less complicated as we and our society have grown more complex.

In romantic pursuits, we too often define our problem as simply a failing to meet the right person. In other words, we see our romantic fate as largely due to luck. This simplistic view of winning love too often leads us to heartbreak. The true nature of "meeting Mr. or Ms. Right" is clarified by recasting romance as a competitive challenge, a comparison of choices, not only for ourselves but for those we do meet. Everyone always has the option of remaining alone, without a romantic partner but few of us prefer that alternative unless all the others options are clearly worse. Most people also have the choice of "settling" for someone that may or may not meet their long-term need.

Romance is never as simple as meeting the right person. All the dating services and websites in the world will not address most people's romantic challenges. We could be meeting Mr. or Ms. Right every day. Our problem is engaging that person in such a way that we can get to know him or her and eventually create a meaningful, lasting relationship with them. This challenge requires a complete set of competitive skills. As someone looking for the best possible partner, our job is decision-making and problem-solving. According to Sun Tzu, all problems in competition are opportunities in disguise. If there were no problems, there would be no opportunities for improvement.

Sun Tzu's strategy insists that we make the most of our strengths to compensate for our weaknesses. Our strengths and weaknesses do not come from our situation alone, but from our relative position within a relationship, or, more precisely, a network of relationships. No one finds lasting romance in a vacuum. To make the right decisions, we must understand the key elements

Foreword: Using Romantic Strategy

that define our strategic position. *The Art of War* was written as a guide to overcoming obstacles. When we are faced with challenges, our natural reactions are "flight" or "fight," running away from a challenge or getting into conflict with people. This is clearly true in romantic relationships, where people think that their only choices are breaking off relationships or fighting with each other to work out the unavoidable problem. This lack of strategic tools is what Sun Tzu's addresses in his work.

The Art of War offers a distinct, nonintuitive system for problem-solving. It solidifies a vague idea of a strategy into a clear, well-defined set of principles. Sun Tzu teaches that only a few key factors define our strategic position. Success goes not to the smartest, sexiest, or most aggressive but to those who best understand their situation and what their alternatives for improving it really are. When we have mastered Sun Tzu's system of strategy, we are able to almost better analyze romantic situations, spot opportunities, and make the appropriate decisions.

This work is translation of a certain set of ideas from a military context to the world of romance. As in all our *Art of War* adaptations, we present our *Art of Love* version side by side with our complete, award-winning translation of the original text of *The Art of War*. We suggest that in reading this work, we read both texts and not just our adaptation for winning love.

Sun Tzu wrote about the psychology of relationships. He wrote about the importance of change, momentum, and a spiritual connection. Human relationships haven't changed in the last two thousand years and won't over the next two thousand. The only differences between modern romantic relationships and the ancient military battles of Sun Tzu's era are the types of tools we use and the battlegrounds on which we compete. There is a reason why romance has been seen as part of the battle of the sexes from the time humanity began recording its progress.

Sun Tzu saw that, at their roots, all competitive challenges are balance costs against rewards. The secret to success, he concluded, is not just winning battles, but winning in a way that minimizes our costs. Difficult relationships that cost either party more than they reward them cannot be sustained. The beauty of human love is that, by its very nature, it can cut our costs and multiply our rewards.

Though Sun Tzu's strategy shows us how to find success in competitive situations, his recipe for success is to avoid unnecessary conflict. He sees such conflict as inherently costly. He teaches us how to handle direct, hostile confrontations when they cannot be avoided, but his basic approach is to defuse these situations before they occur. The approach is psychological: we must convince others to give us what we want without a fight because it is also what they want. We must share our goals to such a degree that a gain for one person does not represent a sacrifice from the other.

Sun Tzu teaches that we must learn to think competitive in all things. This means that we must think about the comparisons that are constantly being made. Biologically speaking, all species are in constant competition for mates and offspring. Those in which we are romantically interests always have alternatives to connecting with us. We must understand their alternatives and appreciate their perspective.

According to Sun Tzu's teaching, we cannot succeed through our own efforts alone. We don't create opportunities. We can defend our existing position in relationships from attack, but the competitive environment itself must provide the opportunities for those relationship to develop. The secret is recognizing these opportunities when they present themselves, and, once we recognize them, we must have the confidence to act. Successful relationships usually require watchful patience. At key times, however, they require instant action. Sun Tzu feels that opportunities are always

Foreword: Using Romantic Strategy

abundant, since every problem creates an opportunity, but that they are very difficult to recognize and act upon.

In addressing the question whether Sun Tzu's methods work in keeping romance alive, I can only share my own experience. Before I learned this approach to seeing life as a comparison of options, I felt trapped in an unhappy marriage. Its problems stemmed from my own insecurities, a poor choice of partner, and my having no sense of how to build a relationship. That marriage ended in divorce.

As I started practicing Sun Tzu's ideas, not only did I become successful in business, but I was able to pursue and win a woman who I would have once considered unattainable. Since then we have gone on to build a relationship that is the closest and strongest partnership I know. We have shared good times and bad, sickness and health and have only grown from the experience of doing it together.

This books serves only as an introduction to Sun Tzu's methods. If you find these ideas interesting, we have developed a number of other works, both books, audios, and on-line courses for mastering these principles. Our most detailed work, the nine volumes of *Sun Tzu's Art of War Playbook,* breaks *The Art of War* down into a series of over 230 articles on the nine areas of strategic skill. To learn more, visit our site, SunTzus.com, the home of the Science of Strategy Institute.

Gary Gagliardi, 2014

♦ ♦ ♦

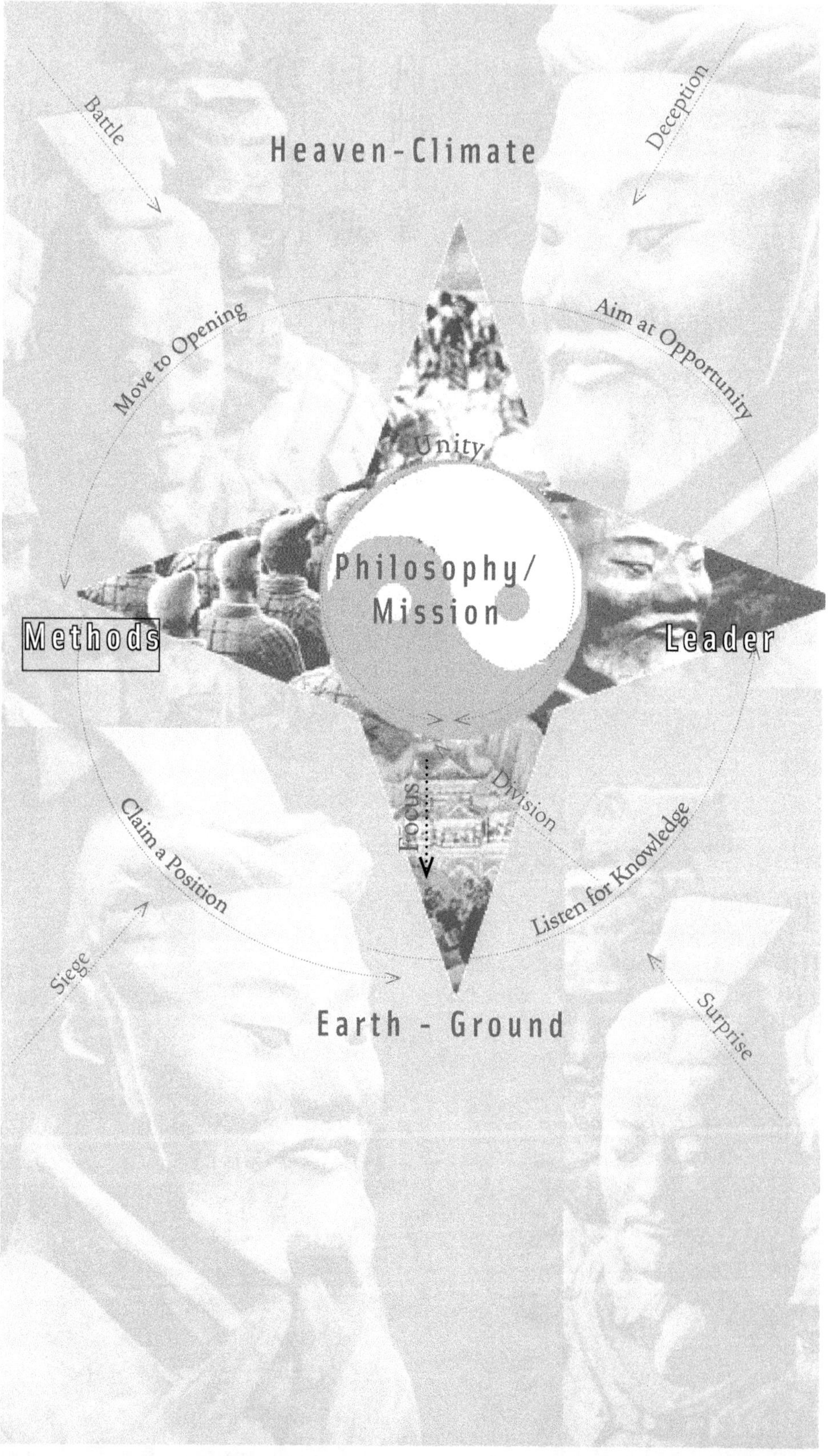

Heaven-Climate

Battle

Deception

Move to Opening

Aim at Opportunity

Unity

Philosophy/ Mission

Methods

Leader

Division

Focus

Claim a Position

Listen for Knowledge

Siege

Surprise

Earth - Ground

Introduction

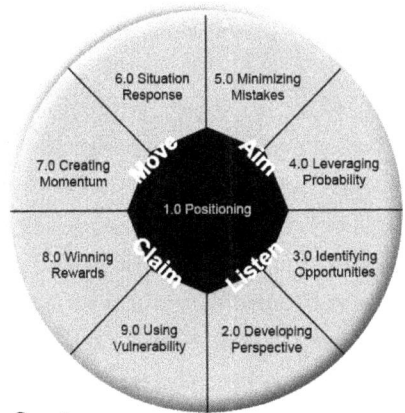

Sun Tzu's Strategic System

This book is for those who want to introduce themselves to the basic principles of Sun Tzu's competitive strategy and apply them to making better romantic decisions. If you are new to Sun Tzu's strategic principles, you will find *The Art of War and The Art of Love* easier to understand if you first familiarize yourself with a few basic concepts, metaphors, and analogies.

Sun Tzu's system is based on the traditions of Chinese science and philosophy and written from that perspective. Those traditions organized ideas around five elements (see facing page) that date back to the *I-Ching* and nine skills (see illustration above), derived from the *Bagua*, that illustrate the eight directions of movement plus the stillness of the center. This introduction gives you an overview of these key components of his strategic system.

Sun Tzu taught that success in competitive environments is not a matter of winning fights with others. Competition is not a fight. Competition is a comparison. This comparison leads to other people making decisions that determine our success.

What is compared is what we call "positions." Success depends on building and advancing strategic positions. Positioning is the core skill in his strategic system.

Sun Tzu defines a position as based on five elements. These five elements—mission, climate, ground, the leader, and methods—define a strategic position and provide our basis for analyzing our positions relative to the positions of others. All the other skills of his toolkit for advancing positions—developing perspective, identifying, opportunities, and so on—develop these elements.

The five elements defining positions are the underlying framework of Sun Tzu's work. However, Sun Tzu did not explain this system because his contemporaries understood it from traditional Chinese philosophy. Instead, his work was written to explain the differences between his elements and those used in traditional Chinese science

Sun Tzu taught that wars of attrition, that is, competitive battles where each competitor tries to tear down the other's position, cannot result in long-term success. Costly battles weaken both contesting parties, opening the way for outside competitors. To avoid wasting resources in such battles, Sun Tzu teaches you how to build positions that others cannot easily challenge and ideally want to join. These lessons are particularly valuable in navigating the uncharted waters of relationships.

The first element that defines a position is what Sun Tzu called *philosophy* and we refer to as *mission*. This Chinese term translated as "philosophy" and "mission" literally means "path". A mission defines the goals and values that guide our progress in any pursuit. Every person has a mission and a purpose that define their personal philosophy. To create a successful relationship, this core philosophy must be shared. You mission must bond with that of your romantic partner. It isn't enough to simply want a relationship. To work, the relationship must serve a shared purpose.

Mission is the basis of two internal characteristics the Sun Tzu describes: *uniting* and *focusing* that create strong relationships. In Sun Tzu's system, both arise directly from your shared goals or mission. *Uniting* holds the relationship together. *Focusing* concentrates your shared efforts in your external goals. Relationships lacking unity and focus are inherently unstable and doomed.

The next two key elements define position within the larger environment. Sun Tzu divides that world into two opposite and yet complementary components, *heaven (climate)* and *ground (earth)*. Heaven and ground define the time and place of your position and your relationships. The importance of the environment is the great insight of Sun Tzu's work. Romance doesn't exist separately from the world except fiction. Real romance takes its shape from the real world.

Sun Tzu taught that most of us view our situations too narrowly. His second key strategic skill defines specific techniques for *Developing Perspective* on our position in the world so that we can see our position as others see us. A strategic position consists both of an objective reality and collection of subjective opinions about that reality. We can change objective reality easily only by first leveraging subjective opinions.

Heaven is the meaning of the Chinese character Sun Tzu used to describes time in terms of uncontrollable and unpredictable change. We usually use the term as "climate" in our training and often "weather" in the translation. The climate arises from trends that change over time. The cycle of the seasons are the most obvious trends in the natural environment, but the world of relationships has its own emotional cycle and romantic climate. People's attitudes and emotions are the key component of climate.

In today's complex social environment, different romantic ideas come in and go out of fashion. The pace of change based on increasing pace of communication forces all individuals to keep up with these changes in romantic climate. This change erodes all existing positions and, at the same time, creates opportunities to advance your position. His third strategic skill uses change for *Identifying Opportunities* in the environment.

Ground is the stable world of reality within the social environment. While fashions change, the basic attraction between the sexes are as old as time. The ground is also the basis for economics within Sun Tzu's system. Economics, the balance of costs and rewards, it based on certain physical realities. Unlike the romantic climate, which is largely beyond our control, the ground is determined by our own choices about where we go and how we meet people. Choosing the places we visit—real or in cyberspace—and utilizing them to meet people are the fourth strategic skill, *Leveraging Probability*, which teaches how different types of ground favors some types of positions over others.

Within the world of relationships, the unique characteristics of our personalities and our abilities are also part of our strategic positions. Sun Tzu breaks these important internal characteristics into two opposite and complementary components: our *leadership* ability and our *methods*.

Decision-making is the unique responsibility of a *leader* in Sun Tzu's system. All people are, in a free society, leaders in their romantic relationships because they must make their own decisions about which relationships to pursue and which to reject. This is not the case in a society of arranged marriages. Leadership is the realm of individual choice and character. A person masters Sun Tzu's strategy so that he or she can make the right decisions quickly.

A successful leader must make the right decisions instinctively. This demands Sun Tzu's fifth and sixth key skills: *Minimizing Mistakes* and *Situation Response*. Minimizing mistakes focuses on a necessary economy of action, preserving our limited resources. Situation response teaches how to choose actions instantly based upon the key conditions of that define a situation.

Methods are the skills of individuals and techniques of group organization. Our success depends upon how well we deal with other people. Methods are the ways in which we interact with others. Generally, all of Sun Tzu's techniques can be described as methods. The literal translation of his books title is "competitive methods."

Standard methods means doing what is expected and acceptable. Good strategy requires going beyond what is expected, innovating methods based on existing ones. Sun Tzu's seventh skill is *Creating Momentum*, which requires combining standards with something new. In relationships, the something new is usually intimacy, which creates momentum in a relationship.

A rewarding relationship is based of the right combination of mission, climate, ground, leadership, and methods. Once we develop a rewarding position, others will try to take it from us. Defending positions is a necessary part of advancing them. It requires Sun Tzu's ninth and final skill, *Understanding Vulnerabilities*.

The Art of War was written to be concise. It starts with its most basic concepts, the five key elements, and then addresses progressively more complex and detailed ideas. Along the way, Sun Tzu tries to correct the most common misunderstandings and mistakes that people made in pursuing success. In doing so, he uses analogies, metaphors, and historical references familiar to those of his time, but often lost on modern readers. We can adapt these references to the challenges in our relationships to capture more of Sun Tzu's meaning.

If you are interested in a learning Sun Tzu's principles in more detail, we refer you to our on-line *Sun Tzu's Warrior's Rule Book*. This work details Sun Tzu's nine skill in terms of 232 interwoven principles. Each of these principles is explained as set of step-by-step rules. Each rule is illustrated by it application to a specific competitive challenge. Some of these challenges are drawn from modern romantic situations.

Chapter 1

Analysis – Research

Comparing people and potential relationships doesn't sound romantic. However, this is what is always really happening in all romantic pursuits. For Sun Tzu, competition means simply comparing alternatives. Romance in a form of competition because it requires a comparison and a choice of what Sun Tzu calls "positions."

Every type of relationship that we can have is a different position. We don't create these "positions" because they arise from the larger world that we cannot control. Before we can act to find love, we must know what our real options are and how they affect our potential for winning love.

Comparing relationships means analyzing alternatives. This analysis begins with the five most important points of comparison. This analysis enables us to understand our relative position. We cannot trust our own view of our situation. This means questioning what we think we know and going outside our normal circles to gather information.

We can never take information for granted. For Sun Tzu, communication is the realm of deception, where people are often either self-deluded or mislead by others. In the end, all relationship analysis is a matter of carefully balancing conflicting information about our position within the arena of our existing and potential relationships. We don't need perfect information to arrive at the best possible decisions about how to move forward. We simply must continually improve our analysis.

The Art of War: **Analysis**

SUN TZU SAID:

This is war. **1**
It is the most important skill in the nation.
It is the basis of life and death.
It is the philosophy of survival or destruction.
You must know it well.

⁶Your skill comes from five factors.
Study these factors when you plan war.
You must insist on knowing your situation.
1. Discuss philosophy.
2. Discuss the climate.
3. Discuss the ground.
4. Discuss leadership.
5. Discuss military methods.

STRATEGY:

Winning is the skill of leveraging positions. Analyze your position by looking at five simple factors.

¹⁴Start with your military philosophy.
Command your people in a way that gives them a higher shared purpose.
You can lead them to death.
You can lead them to life.
They must never fear danger or dishonesty.

The Art of Love: **Finding Love**

A LOVE SEEKER HEARS:

1 This is love.
It is the key to all happiness in life.
It is the foundation of prosperity or poverty.
It is the path to growth or stagnation.
We must understand winning love well.

Our ability to find love comes from five elements.
Evaluate these elements when looking for love.
We must know:

1. Our beliefs
2. Our attitude
3. Our environment
4. Our character
5. Our skills at building relationships.

Winning true love begins with our personal beliefs.
Good mates are attracted to those who want a higher, shared purpose
Romance requires sacrifice.
Romance requires achievement.
Others must not fear danger or dishonesty from us.

MISSION:

Mission is the core of your position. A clear mission creates strength and focus in your relationship.

The Art of War: Analysis

POSITION:

Your position exists within a larger competitive environment, which you do not control.

[19] Next, you have the climate.
It can be sunny or overcast.
It can be hot or cold.
It includes the timing of the seasons.

[23] Next is the terrain.
It can be distant or near.
It can be difficult or easy.
It can be open or narrow.
It also determines your life or death.

[28] Next is the commander.
He must be smart, trustworthy, caring, brave, and strict.

[30] Finally, you have your military methods.
They include the shape of your organization.
This comes from your management philosophy.
You must master their use.

DECISION:

Good strategic decisions are based on seeing how these five factors together create your position.

[34] All five of these factors are critical.
As a commander, you must pay attention to them.
Understanding them brings victory.
Ignoring them means defeat.

The Art of Love: Finding Love

Next is our attitude.
We can be optimistic or pessimistic.
We can be positive or negative.
We must recognize that our attitude changes over time.

Next is our environment.
It can isolate us or bring us together with others.
It can make it difficult or easy to get to know people.
It can include many contacts or limit us to a few people.
It determines our success or failure at winning love.

Next is our character.
We must be witty, dependable, caring, courageous, and self-disciplined.

Finally, we must have the skills for building relationships.
This includes organizing our lives to include others.
Our skills arise from our true beliefs.
We must work to develop our relationship skills.

All five of these elements are important.
We must evaluate them in ourselves and others.
Our success in love depends on them.
Ignoring them leads to heartbreak.

> **VISION:**
>
> *Your ability to foresee and leverage changes in the relationship is the key to your romantic success.*

> **LEVERAGE:**
>
> *Your unique opportunities for love come from your unique position within the larger environment.*

The Art of War: Analysis

You must learn through analysis. **2**
You must question the situation.

³You must ask:
Which government has the right philosophy?
Which commander has the skill?
Which season and place has the advantage?
Which method of command works?
Which group of forces has the strength?
Which officers and men have the training?
Which rewards and punishments make sense?
This tells when you will win and when you will lose.
Some commanders perform this analysis.
If you use these commanders, you will win.
Keep them.
Some commanders ignore this analysis.
If you use these commanders, you will lose.
Get rid of them.

Plan an advantage by listening. **3**
Adjust to your situation.
Get assistance from the outside.
Influence events.
Then analysis can find opportunities and give you control.

RELATIVITY:

No position is good or bad in itself. You only understand positions by comparing them to others.

The Art of Love: **Finding Love**

2 Winning love requires finding the right person..
We must look at people objectively.

We must ask these questions:
Which people have compatible beliefs?
Do they have the right kind of character?
When and where can we meet these people?
Which dating technique works best?
In which groups are we likely to find the right person?
How well have we prepared our minds and bodies?
What behaviors are positive, and what behaviors are risky?
This questioning shows us how likely we are to find love.
Some people are honest enough to ask these questions.
If you are one of these people, you will find love.
Keep at it.
Most people do not look at the facts objectively.
If you are one of them, your relationships are doomed.
You must change.

3 We find love by listening to other people.
Listening makes us attractive.
Get introductions from others.
Know how you look to others.
Searching for love uncovers our strengths and weaknesses.

> **MYOPIA:**
>
> *If you fail to get an outside perspective on your position, you will miss most romantic opportunities.*

The Art of War: **Analysis**

4
Warfare is one thing.
It is a philosophy of deception.

³When you are ready, you try to appear incapacitated.
When active, you pretend inactivity.
When you are close to the enemy, you appear distant.
When far away, you pretend you are near.

⁷If the enemy has a strong position, entice him away from it.
If the enemy is confused, be decisive.
If the enemy is solid, prepare against him.
If the enemy is strong, avoid him.
If the enemy is angry, frustrate him.
If the enemy is weaker, make him arrogant.
If the enemy is relaxed, make him work.
If the enemy is united, break him apart.
Attack him when he is unprepared.
Leave when he least expects it.

¹⁷You will find a place where you can win.
You cannot first signal your intentions.

CONTROL:

Winning begins and ends with the power of information. You control others by controlling their perceptions.

The Art of Love: **Finding Love**

4 Romance is one thing:
It is a method of controlling perceptions.

If we are infatuated, we try to appear indifferent.
If we want to impress someone, we try to appear at ease.
When we want to be close, we try to appear distant.
When distracted, we try to appear interested.

If we want someone's attention, we must entice them.
If they are confused, we must help them decide.
If they are hard to know, we must work at it.
If they are married, we must avoid getting involved.
If we make them angry, we must tease them.
If they are uncertain, we must make them confident.
If they take us for granted, we must make them work.
If we are locked out, we must break in.
We must ask for a date when others are unprepared.
We must leave relationships when they are going nowhere.

You can find a true, lifelong love.
Never pass it by.

> **APPEAL:**
>
> *You can only be the best possible you, and you cannot pretend to be who you are not without inviting trouble.*

The Art of War: **Analysis**

Manage to avoid battle until your organization can **5** count on certain victory.
You must calculate many advantages.
Before you go to battle, your organization's analysis can indicate that you may not win.
You can count few advantages.
Many advantages add up to victory.
Few advantages add up to defeat.
How can you know your advantages without analyzing them?
We can see where we are by means of our observations.
We can foresee our victory or defeat by planning.

PATIENCE:

Consciously choosing not to act is just as important as acting decisively when the time is right.

The Art of Love: **Finding Love**

5 We must avoid making or asking for commitments until we are sure the relationship makes sense.

We must have many of the same interests.

Before getting into a relationship, we must avoid commitments on relationships that cannot last.

We can foresee problems with relationships.

Sharing many interests and goals adds up to romantic success.

Conflicts and incompatibility add up to a broken heart.

How can we love without searching for the right person?

We know our situation by observing it honestly.

We can predict romance or heartbreak by thinking about it.

CHOICES:

You advance your love life by investing in relationships where these five aspects are in your favor.

Related Articles from *Sun Tzu's Playbook*

In this first chapter, Sun Tzu introduces the basics of positioning. We explore these ideas in more detail in our Sun Tzu's Art of War Playbook. *To learn the step-by-step techniques for positioning, we recommend the* Playbook *articles listed below.*

1.0.0 Strategic Positioning: developing relatively superior positions.

1.1.0 Position Paths: the continuity of strategic positions over time.

1.1.1 Position Dynamics: how all current positions evolve over time.

1.1.2 Defending Positions: defending current positions until new positions are established.

1.2 Subobjective Positions: the subjective and objective aspects of a position.

1.2.1 Competitive Landscapes: the arenas in which rivals jockey for position.

1.2.2 Exploiting Exploration: how competitive landscapes are searched and positions identified.

1.2.3 Position Complexity: how positions arise from interactions in complex environments.

1.3 Elemental Analysis: the relevant components of all competitive positions.

1.3.1 Competitive Comparison: competition as the comparison of positions.

1.3.2 Element Scalability: how elements of a position scale up to larger positions.

1.4 The External Environment: external conditions shaping strategic positions.

1.4.1 Climate Shift: forces of environmental change shaping temporary conditions.

1.4.2 Ground Features: the persistent resources that we can control.

1.5 Competing Agents: the key characteristics of competitors.

1.5.1 Command Leadership: individual decision-making.

1.5.2. Group Methods: systems for executing decisions.

1.6 Mission Values: the goals and values needed for motivation.

1.6.1 Shared Mission: finding goals that others can share.

1.6.2 Types of Motivations: hierarchies of motivation that define missions.

1.6.3 Shifting Priorities: how missions change according to temporary conditions.

Chapter 2

Going to War – Rewarding Relationships

The world of relationships consists of costs and benefits and Sun Tzu's strategy is based on balancing them. His strategy comes down to knowing how to "make victory pay." The time to think about this balance is before you get into relationships. Relationship costs go far beyond financial. It isn't enough simply having a relationship. You must make sure that relationship satisfies needs.

There are risks inherent in every investment of time and effort. Time invested in the wrong relationships is time lost forever. Many people are driven by optimism, but the costs and rewards of a relationships are unpredictable. While popular culture makes it seem that relationships are risk-free, this is not what most people experience. Bad relationships can be deeply costly.

Your ability to control costs is the key to making relationships rewarding. You cannot invest in every relationship as though you are certain that this person is going to be the love of your life. You cannot know costs and rewards at the beginning of any relationship. You certainly cannot know what other people's expectations are concerning their own costs and rewards. You may enjoy another person's company, but you cannot know what that can cost you in the future.

Costs never control themselves. This is where your decision-making skills are necessary. You want every relationship to be rewarding as directly and quickly as possible.

The Art of War: Going to War

SUN TZU SAID:

Everything depends on your use of military philosophy. 1
Moving the army requires thousands of vehicles.
These vehicles must be loaded thousands of times.
The army must carry a huge supply of arms.
You need ten thousand acres of grain.
This results in internal and external shortages.
Any army consumes resources like an invader.
It uses up glue and paint for wood.
It requires armor for its vehicles.
People complain about the waste of a vast amount of metal.
It will set you back when you attempt to raise tens of thousands of troops.

ECONOMY:

Strategy teaches that the key to success is making good decisions about using limited resources.

[12]Using a huge army makes war costly to win.
Long delays create a dull army and sharp defeats.
Attacking enemy cities drains your forces.
Long violent campaigns that exhaust the nation's resources are wrong.

The Art of Love: Rewarding Relationships

A LOVE SEEKER HEARS:

1 Success in finding love requires faith.
Searching for love requires meeting many people.
Getting to know those people is hard work.
We must develop our interpersonal skills.
We must invest time and effort.
We must risk both our internal and external equilibrium.
Nothing consumes our lives like our relationships.
Relationships require creativity and imagination.
They require that we protect ourselves.
People should always fear the risks of a serious commitment to the wrong person.
Still, we will never find true love by continually looking for new conquests.

Multiple relationships make it difficult to find love.
Committing to a bad relationship leads to heartbreak.
Conflict in our relationships drains our energy.
Long, drawn out courtships that demand all our efforts are wrong.

QUICKNESS:

You cannot know where a relationship will go before it goes there. Work at moving relationships forward.

The Art of War: **Going to War**

AGGRESSION:

Going slowly and "carefully" is more costly and dangerous than moving forward.

[16]Manage a dull army.
You will suffer sharp defeats.
Drain your forces.
Your money will be used up.
Your rivals will multiply as your army collapses
and they will begin against you.
It doesn't matter how smart you are.
You cannot get ahead by taking losses!

[23]You hear of people going to war too quickly.
Still, you won't see a skilled war that lasts a long time.

[25]You can fight a war for a long time or you can make your nation strong.
You can't do both.

2

Make no assumptions about all the dangers in using military force.
Then you won't make assumptions about the benefits of using arms either.

SMALL IS FAST:

Speed is closely connected to size. Do not mistake costly size for power and safety.

[3]You want to make good use of war.
Do not raise troops repeatedly.
Do not carry too many supplies.
Choose to be useful to your nation.
Feed off the enemy.
Make your army carry only the provisions it needs.

The Art of Love: Rewarding Relationships

Get stuck in a dead-end relationship.
Your faith in love will fade.
Get stuck in a one-sided relationship.
Your patience will be exhausted.
As your enthusiasm fades, your insecurities will undermine your confidence.
It does not matter how smart you are.
You cannot find love in a bad relationship.

> MOMENTUM:
>
> *If a romantic relationship does not constantly advance, it will eventually far apart.*

You can sometimes move too quickly toward marriage.
However, you won't win love by dragging out bad matches.

You can stay in dead-end relationship for a long time, or you can find love.
You can't have it both ways.

2 You can never understand all of the risks in meeting a new person.
Nor can you know all the possibilities in meeting a new person either.

You must act wisely in searching for love.
Do not repeat the same mistakes.
Do not accumulate emotional baggage.
Choose to be serious about your future.
Find rewarding relationships.
Get involved only with people who make you give you what you need.

> TESTING:
>
> *Each small move into a new relationship is a test to see how quickly you can find each other..*

The Art of War: **Going to War**

3 The nation impoverishes itself shipping to troops that are far away.
Distant transportation is costly for hundreds of families.
Buying goods with the army nearby is also expensive.
High prices also exhaust wealth.
If you exhaust your wealth, you then quickly hollow out your military.
Military forces consume a nation's wealth entirely.
War leaves households in the former heart of the nation with nothing.

[8]War destroys hundreds of families.
Out of every ten families, war leaves only seven.
War empties the government's storehouses.
Broken armies will get rid of their horses.
They will throw down their armor, helmets, and arrows.
They will lose their swords and shields.
They will leave their wagons without oxen.
War will consume 60 percent of everything you have.

4 Because of this, it is the intelligent commander's duty to feed off the enemy.

[2]Use a cup of the enemy's food.
It is worth twenty of your own.
Win a bushel of the enemy's feed.
It is worth twenty of your own.

OPPONENTS:

Strategy demands that you deplete any resources that would naturally go to your competitors.

The Art of Love: **Rewarding Relationships**

3 We waste our limited time in relationships with people who live far away.
Long-distance relationships seldom work.
Indifferent, convenient relationships are also costly.
They steal away the time needed to find love.
Relationships that require constant effort to maintain will exhaust you.
Churning through relationships will make you entirely cynical.
Lovers who are not committed to building a life together leave you a broken heart.

Romantic competition destroys many families.
Half of all marriages end in divorce.
Divorce takes away everything we have.
Broken marriages tear families apart.
Partners have to sell their cars, furniture, and houses.
They have to deal with lawyers and courts.
They leave their children without a parent.
Divorce destroys everything that is truly valuable.

4 Because love is costly, we must develop relationships that sustain mutually us.

Find someone who respects you.
Respect lasts twenty times longer than infatuation.
Find someone who cares about you.
Caring is worth twenty times more than attraction.

> **RESULTS:**
>
> *Choose potential partners from those with whom you can quickly find mutual companionship and respect.*

The Art of War: **Going to War**

⁶You can kill the enemy and frustrate him as well.
Take the enemy's strength from him by stealing away his money.

⁸Fight for the enemy's supply wagons.
Capture his supplies by using overwhelming force.
Reward the first who capture them.
Then change their banners and flags.
Mix them in with your own wagons to increase your supply line.
Keep your soldiers strong by providing for them.
This is what it means to beat the enemy while you grow more powerful.

Make victory in war pay for itself. **5**
Avoid expensive, long campaigns.
The military commander's knowledge is the key.
It determines if the civilian officials can govern.
It determines if the nation's households are peaceful or a danger to the state.

♦ ♦ ♦

MAKE IT PAY:

Success is defined only by its profitability.

The Art of Love: **Rewarding Relationships**

You can win love and avoid heartbreak as well.
Build good relationships by spending time with people who nurture you.

Search to find someone with a caring nature.
We must commit everything when we find the right person.
We reward ourselves by winning his or her love.
We must make our commitments visible.
We must be able to join our supporters with those who support are lover.
We keep relationships strong by nurturing them.
This is what it means to overcome life's difficulties together to grow stronger relationhships.

5 A good relationship should support itself.
Avoid long-lasting, costly, empty relationships.
Our knowledge of people is the key.
It determines our ability to make good decisions.
It determines if our relationships are successful or headed for failure.

CAMPAIGNS:

Find solid relationships that can grow.

2 The Art of Love   45

Related Articles from *Sun Tzu's Playbook*

In his second chapter, Sun Tzu teaches basic competitive economics. We explore these ideas in more detail in our **Sun Tzu's Art of War Playbook**. *To learn the step-by-step techniques for economical political campaigning, we recommend the articles listed below.*

1.3.1 Competitive Comparison: competition as the comparison of positions.

1.6.1 Shared Mission: finding goals that others can share.

1.8.3 Cycle Time: speed in feedback and reaction.

1.8.4 Probabilistic Process: the role of chance in strategic processes and systems.

2.2.1 Personal Relationships: how information depends on personal relationships.

2.2.2 Mental Models: how mental models simplify decision-making.

2.3.4 Using Questions: using questions in gathering information and predicting reactions.

3.1 Strategic Economics: balancing the cost and benefits of positioning.

3.1.1 Resource Limitations: the inherent limitation of strategic resources.

3.1.2 Strategic Profitability: understanding gains and losses.

3.1.3 Conflict Cost: the costly nature of resolving competitive comparisons by conflict.

3.1.4 Openings: seeking openings to avoid costly conflict.

3.1.5 Unpredictable Value: the limitations of predicting the value of positions.

3.1.6 Time Limitations: the time limits on opportunities.

4.0 Leveraging Probability: better decisions regarding our choice of opportunities.

4.1 Future Potential: the limitations and potential of current and future positions.

4.2 Choosing Non-Action: choosing between action and non-action.

5.3 Reaction Time: the use of speed in choosing actions.

5.3.1 Speed and Quickness: the use of pace within a dynamic environment.

5.3.2 Opportunity Windows: the effect of speed upon opposition.

5.3.3 Information Freshness: choosing actions based on freshness of information.

5.4 Minimizing Action: minimizing waste, i.e., less is more.

5.4.1 Testing Value : choosing actions to test for value.

5.4.2 Successful Mistakes: learning from our mistakes.

5.5 Focused Power: size consideration in safe experimentation.

5.5.1 Force Size: limiting the size of force in an advance.

5.5.2 Distance Limitations: the use of short steps to reach distant goals.

Chapter 3

Planning Attacks — Looking for Love

For Sun Tzu, "attacking" means moving into new areas. Where do you go to find relationships? Singles bars? The internet? Church? For Sun Tzu, the question of where is not as important as how. The chief issues in moving into new areas are unity and focus. A successful campaign is one that unites you with others. It is one that is focused on a clear goal, Focus and unity are connected ideas. You can not be focused if you are trying to be all things to all people.

The shared values of mission are the key. When it comes to building relationships, we should share at many different levels to create unity. This sharing creates focus. Through sharing, others gain our attention, and we gain the attention of others. Focus and unity create strength in relationships. In Sun Tzu, the chief value of strength is not just to win battles but to prevent them.

The opposite of unity and focus is conflict. You must pursue new relationship that minimize conflict. The worst way to build a relationship is to directly attack someone we see as a rival. Conflict destroy unity. It is an affront to focus.

The Art of Love uses an incremental approach to success. You must set up small, focused encounters as the basis of comparison. You must choose situations in which you look good. The relative strength of your position determines how aggressive you are.

Knowledge determines your ability to unite and concentrate your car. It is always dangerous to miscalculate the relative strength of your organization in facing a competitor.

The Art of War: **Planning Attacks**

UNITY:

Strategy teaches that the size of an organization is not nearly as important as how united it is.

SUN TZU SAID:

Everyone relies on the arts of war. 1
A united nation is strong.
A divided nation is weak.
A united army is strong.
A divided army is weak.
A united force is strong.
A divided force is weak.
United men are strong.
Divided men are weak.
A united unit is strong.
A divided unit is weak.

[12]Unity works because it enables you to win every battle you fight.
Still, this is the foolish goal of a weak leader.
Avoid battle and make the enemy's men surrender.
This is the right goal for a superior leader.

The best way to make war is to ruin the enemy's plans. 2
The next best is to disrupt alliances.
The next best is to attack the opposing army.
The worst is to attack the enemy's cities.

The Art of Love: **Looking for Love**

A LOVE SEEKER HEARS:

1 Every relationship emerges from attraction.
Shared values make a relationship strong.
Differing values make a relationship weak.
Shared moments build a relationship.
Moments apart divide a relationship.
Similar goals cement a relationship.
Separate goals break a relationship.
Devoted people create relationships.
Unfaithful people destroy relationships.
A close relationship is strong.
A distant relationship is weak.

If we are strongly attracted to each other, we can overcome difficulties in our relationship.
But overcoming difficulties isn't enough.
Avoid difficulties and make it easy to agree.
This is the true basis for lasting love.

2 It is best to find someone who is looking for a relationship.
The next best is someone who is dating many people.
The next best is someone in an uncommitted relationship.
The worst is to get involved with someone who is married.

FOCUS:

Unity depends upon shared set of goals that can become a shared life's mission.

The Art of War: **Planning Attacks**

ATTACKS:

In Sun Tzu, an attack is any movement or invasion of a new territory, not fighting with others.

⁵This is what happens when you attack a city.
You can attempt it, but you can't finish it.
First you must make siege engines.
You need the right equipment and machinery.
It takes three months and still you cannot win.
Then you try to encircle the area.
You use three more months without making progress.
Your command still doesn't succeed and this angers you.
You then try to swarm the city.
This kills a third of your officers and men.
You are still unable to draw the enemy out of the city.
This attack is a disaster.

Make good use of war. 3
Make the enemy's troops surrender.
You can do this fighting only minor battles.
You can draw their men out of their cities.
You can do it with small attacks.
You can destroy the men of a nation.
You must keep your campaign short.

DECISION:

Good strategic decisions are based on seeing how these five factors together create your position.

⁸You must use total war, fighting with everything you have.
Never stop fighting when at war.
You can gain complete advantage.
To do this, you must plan your strategy of attack.

The Art of Love: **Looking for Love**

What happens in an affair with a married person?
You can hope for a divorce, but it will never happen.
First, you believe their marriage is broken
You trust that it is just a matter of time and legalities.
This goes on for months, and nothing changes.
You then try to win more of a commitment.
After more months of wasted time, the relationship goes nowhere.
You will make demands but the failure to win commitment angers you.
You then attack the current spouse directly.
This costs you heartbreak and self-respect.
You are still unable to draw the married person out of the relationship.
This type of advance is disastrous.

> DISASTER:
>
> *Simply copying the style and moves of others can win attention but it is a disaster when it comes to a relationship.*

3 Make happy use of love.
We must make others surrender to us.
We do this by overcoming only minor resistance.
We must draw people out of their shell.
We can do it with small sacrifices.
We can overcome a poor opinion of us.
We must keep our courtship subtle.

In winning love, we commit everything to building a relationship.
Never stop paying attention to your beloved.
You can win anyone over.
To do this, you must analyze your romantic progress.

> LEVERAGE:
>
> *You build your reputation in a group a little at a time. Avoid making a big deal about yourself..*

The Art of War: **Planning Attacks**

¹²The rules for making war are:
If you outnumber enemy forces ten to one, surround them.
If you outnumber them five to one, attack them.
If you outnumber them two to one, divide them.
If you are equal, then find an advantageous battle.
If you are fewer, defend against them.
If you are much weaker, evade them.

¹⁹Small forces are not powerful.
However, large forces cannot catch them.

You must master command. 4
The nation must support you.

³Supporting the military makes the nation powerful.
Not supporting the military makes the nation weak.

⁵The army's position is made more difficult by politicians in three different ways.
Ignorant of a military division's inability to advance, they order an advance.
Ignorant of a military division's inability to withdraw, they order a withdrawal.
We call this tying up the army.
They don't understands a military division's function.
Still, they think they can govern military divisions.
This confuses the army's officers.

The Art of Love: **Looking for Love**

Here are the rules for winning love:
If our romantic target is infatuated, we get involved.
If they are impressed, we tease them.
If they are interested, we make them jealous.
If they are indifferent, we make them laugh.
If they are negative, we defend ourselves.
If they are hostile, we avoid them.

Not everyone is attracted to us.
In those situations, we must not pursue them.

4 We must make our own romantic decisions.
Our family must support us.

Encouraging romance strengthens a family's ties.
Families that discourage romantic relationships are weak.

Parents create problems for their children's romances in three different ways.
Ignorant of our needs in a relationship, they pressure us to get involved too soon.
Ignorant of our commitments, they try to break up our relationships.
This hamstrings our romantic efforts.
Parents do not understand how to manage our love life.
Still, they think that they can make better decisions than we can.
This only confuses our ability to decide.

The Art of War: **Planning Attacks**

¹²Politicians don't know the military division of authority.
They think all military divisions are the same.
This will create distrust among the army's officers.

¹⁵The entire army becomes confused and distrusting.
This invites invasion by many different rivals.
We say correctly that disorder in an army kills victory.

You must know five things to win: 5
Victory comes from knowing when to attack and when to avoid battle.
Victory comes from correctly using both large and small forces.
Victory comes from everyone sharing the same goals.
Victory comes from finding opportunities in problems.
Victory comes from having a capable commander and the government leaving him alone.
You must know these five things.
You then know the theory of victory.

We say: 6
"Know yourself and know your enemy.
You will be safe in every battle.
You may know yourself but not know the enemy.
You will then lose one battle for every one you win.
You may not know yourself or the enemy.
You will then lose every battle."

The Art of Love: **Looking for Love**

Family members do not understand our heart's priorities.
They think all romantic relationships are like their own.
This make us distrust our feelings.

Our relationships can become uncertain and insecure.
This invites problems in any romance.
Uncertainty destroys our chances for love.

5 We must know five things to win love:
Success comes from knowing when to pursue a relationship and when to give it time.
Success comes from being comfortable sharing large and small experiences.
Success comes from having the same goals.
Success comes from turning doubts into trust.
Success comes from learning to make our own decisions and our family leaving us alone.
We must know these five things.
We then know the philosophy of winning love.

6 Experience tells us:
We must know ourselves and know our romantic partner.
We will then be safe in our relationship.
We may know ourselves but not our partner.
We will then get half of what we need to succeed.
We may know neither ourself nor our partner.
Then, we will suffer in every relationship.

Related Articles from *Sun Tzu's Playbook*

In this third chapter, Sun Tzu introduces the basics of advancing into new areas. To learn the step-by-step techniques involved, we recommend the Sun Tzu's Art of War Playbook *articles listed below.*

1.1.1 Position Dynamics: how all current positions are always getting better or worse.

1.1.2 Defending Positions: how we defend our current positions until new positions are established.

1.2 Subobjective Positions: the subjective and objective aspects of a position.

1.3.1 Competitive Comparison: competition as the comparison of positions.

1.7 Competitive Power: the sources of superiority in challenges.

1.7.1 Team Unity: strength by joining with others.

1.7.2 Goal Focus: strength as arising from concentrating efforts.

1.8 Progress Cycle: the adaptive loop by which positions are advanced.

1.8.1 Creation and Destruction: the creation and destruction of competitive positions.

1.8.2 The Adaptive Loop: the continual reiteration of position analysis.

2.3.6 Promises and Threats: the use of promises and threats as strategic moves.

2.4 Contact Networks: the range of contacts needed to create perspective.

2.4.1 Ground Perspective: getting information on a new competitive arena.

2.4.2 Climate Perspective: getting perspective on temporary external conditions.

3.0.0 Identifying Opportunities: the use of opportunities to advance a position.

3.1.3 Conflict Cost: the costly nature of resolving competitive comparisons by conflict.

3.2 Opportunity Creation: how change creates opportunities.

3.2.2 Opportunity Invisibility: why opportunities are always hidden.

3.2.4 Emptiness and Fullness: the transformations between strength and weakness.

3.4 Dis-Economies of Scale: how opportunities are created by the size of others.

3.4.2 Opportunity Fit: finding new opportunities that fit your size.

3.4.3 Reaction Lag: how size creates temporary openings.

3.5 Strength and Weakness: openings created by the strength of others.

3.6 Leveraging Subjectivity: openings between subjective and objective positions.

3.7 Defining the Ground: redefining a competitive arena to create relative mismatches.

5.6 Defensive Advances: balancing defending and advancing positions.

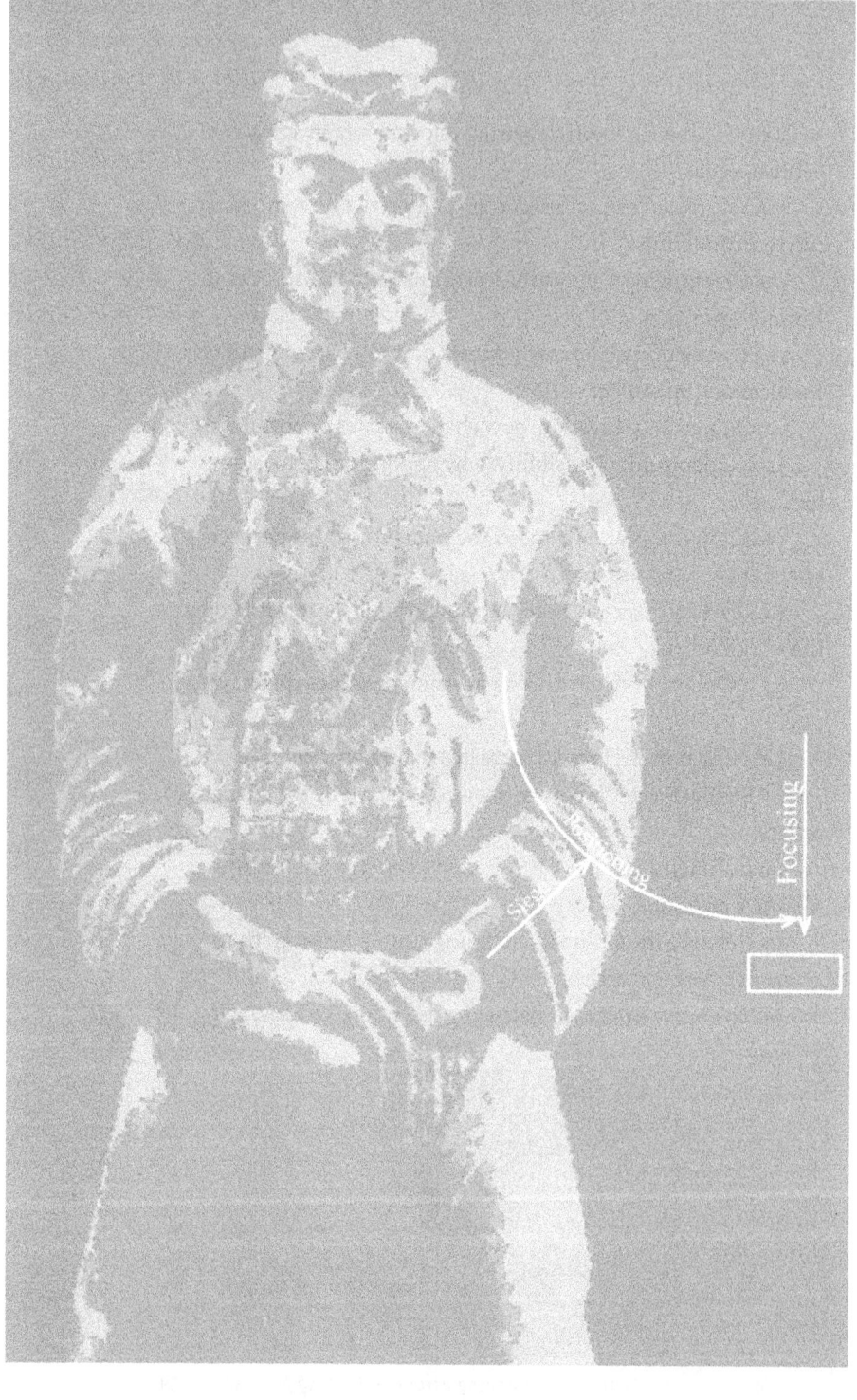

Chapter 4

Positioning – Getting Closer

Wise people know how to take what they are given. According to Sun Tzu's principles of strategy, you do not create your opportunities for getting closer to someone. You can only take advantage of the opportunities that others create for you. Too many people do not know how to recognize these opportunities or what to do with them when they arise. This chapter addresses those skills.

On your own, you can do no more than justify your existing relationship with someone. Only the flow of events can create new opportunities for you. Such opportunities are stepping-stones toward closer relationships, but the other person's feelings must create those stepping-stones before you can move along them.

New opportunities do not come on any schedule. You cannot plan them. Because of this, you must know how to protect your existing relationships until opportunities to get closer appear.

Recognizing a good opportunity and using it to get closer is just the beginning. You must know how to move from into relationships of greater intimacy. You must also know how to make that intimacy rewarding for both of you once you have established it.

A simple formula tells you whether or not it is likely that you can build a closer relationship with someone. Our emotions capture ideas that we cannot put into words, but they are not random. Feelings arise from how compatible your personalities, world views, and goals for the future really are. These deeper realities generate the right emotions in your companion.

The Art of War: **Positioning**

DEFENSE:

Strategy dictates that you must first make sure that your existing position is secure before moving to a new one.

SUN TZU SAID:

Learn from the history of successful battles. 1
Your first actions should deny victory to the enemy.
You pay attention to your enemy to find the way to win.
You alone can deny victory to the enemy.
Only your enemy can allow you to win.

6You must fight well.
You can prevent the enemy's victory.
You cannot win unless the enemy enables your victory.

9We say:
You see the opportunity for victory; you don't create it.

The Art of Love: **Getting Closer**

A LOVE SEEKER HEARS:

1 Learn from the example of successful relationships.
We must first preserve our existing friendship.
We then look for ways to become more intimate.
We alone can preserve the existing relationship.
Only our partner creates the opportunity to get closer.

We must be a trustworthy friend.
We can prevent any relationship from ending.
We can only get closer when the other person is ready.

The truth is simple.
People must discover their feelings; we cannot force them.

OPENINGS:

You must take advantage of the opportunities that arise in the relationship that situations create for you.

The Art of War: **Positioning**

You are sometimes unable to win. 2
You must then defend.
You will eventually be able to win.
You must then attack.
Defend when you have insufficient strength.
Attack when you have a surplus of strength.

⁷You must defend yourself well.
Save your forces and dig in.
You must attack well.
Move your forces when you have a clear advantage.

¹¹You must always protect yourself until you can completely triumph.

Some may see how to win. 3
However, they cannot position their forces where they must.
This demonstrates limited ability.

⁴Some can struggle to a victory and the whole world may praise their winning.
This also demonstrates a limited ability.

⁶Win as easily as picking up a fallen hair.
Don't use all of your forces.
See the time to move.
Don't try to find something clever.
Hear the clap of thunder.
Don't try to hear something subtle.

The Art of Love: **Getting Closer**

2 We cannot always move the relationship forward.
We must then maintain the friendship.
We may eventually discover a more intimate relationship.
We must then take advantage of the opportunity.
Value what you have until the attraction grows stronger.
Invite greater intimacy when the attraction is irresistible.

You must be reliable as a friend.
Relax and get comfortable.
You must be open to more.
Take the next step when the opportunity arises.

You must protect your existing relationship until a closer one is certain.

3 We may know the relationship that we would like.
We may not get an opportunity to build that relationship.
This shows limited ability.

We may find ourselves struggling in our attempts to get closer to someone.
This also shows limited ability.

Move toward closer relationships effortlessly.
Avoid making yourself look foolish.
Wait for the right time.
Do not try to be too clever.
Learn to listen to what your partner says.
Do not imagine what his or her feeling are.

The Art of War: Positioning

¹²Learn from the history of successful battles.
Victory goes to those who make winning easy.
A good battle is one that you will obviously win.
It doesn't take intelligence to win a reputation.
It doesn't take courage to achieve success.

¹⁷You must win your battles without effort.
Avoid difficult struggles.
Fight when your position must win.
You always win by preventing your defeat.

²¹You must engage only in winning battles.
Position yourself where you cannot lose.
Never waste an opportunity to defeat your enemy.

²⁴You win a war by first assuring yourself of victory.
Only afterward do you look for a fight.
Outmaneuver the enemy before the first battle and then fight to win.

BATTLE:

In classical strategy, battle means meeting an opponent's challenge, not necessarily a fight.

The Art of Love: **Getting Closer**

Learn from those who have developed lasting relationships.
People love those who make caring easy.
A good relationship is one that will obviously grow.
We don't have to be a genius to have someone love us.
We do not have to be brave to win love.

We want to develop relationships without pressure.
Avoid stormy relationships.
Create shared experiences that win affection.
We can win love if we avoid rejection.

We win love by first knowing that we are lovable.
Never put yourself in a position where you can be rejected.
Never pass up an opportunity to get closer.

We win love by first assuring ourselves of affection.
Only then do we look for intimacy.
Win your way into someone's heart and then become intimate from love.

> IDENTITY:
>
> *People need to know who you are but only in terms of what you can do to meet their needs.*

The Art of War: **Positioning**

You must make good use of war. 4
Study military philosophy and the art of defense.
You can control your victory or defeat.

⁴This is the art of war:
"1. Discuss the distances.
2. Discuss your numbers.
3. Discuss your calculations.
4. Discuss your decisions.
5. Discuss victory.

¹⁰The ground determines the distance.
The distance determines your numbers.
Your numbers determine your calculations.
Your calculations determine your decisions.
Your decisions determine your victory."

¹⁵Creating a winning war is like balancing a coin of gold
against a coin of silver.
Creating a losing war is like balancing a coin of silver
against a coin of gold.

Winning a battle is always a matter of people. 5
You pour them into battle like a flood of
water pouring into a deep gorge.
This is a matter of positioning.

The Art of Love: **Getting Closer**

4 We must leverage all romance.
We must understand our desires and protect ourselves.
We alone determine our success or heartbreak.

This is the art of love.
     1. Discuss your differences.
     2. Discuss your compatibility.
     3. Discuss your feelings.
     4. Discuss your future.
     5. Discuss commitment.

Our backgrounds determine our differences.
Our differences determine our compatibility.
Our compatibility determines our feelings.
Our feelings determine our future.
Our future determines our commitment.

Winning love means caring more about our partner's happiness than our own.
Losing love means caring more about our own passions than those of our partner.

5 Winning love always depends upon a person's feelings.
When you find the right person, everything flows together easily.
This is a matter of relationship.

✦ ✦ ✦

Related Articles from *Sun Tzu's Playbook*

In this fourth chapter, Sun Tzu explains the process for advancing positions. To learn the step-by-step techniques involved, we recommend the Sun Tzu's Art of War Playbook articles listed below.

1.1.2 Defending Positions: how we defend our current positions until new positions are established.

1.2 Subobjective Positions: the subjective and objective aspects of a position.

1.3.1 Competitive Comparison: competition as the comparison of positions.

1.7 Competitive Power: the sources of superiority in challenges.

1.8 Progress Cycle: the adaptive loop by which positions are advanced.

1.8.1 Creation and Destruction: the creation and destruction of competitive positions.

1.8.2 The Adaptive Loop: the continual reiteration of position analysis.

3.0.0 Identifying Opportunities: the use of opportunities to advance a position.

3.2 Opportunity Creation: how change creates opportunities.

3.2.4 Emptiness and Fullness: the transformations between strength and weakness.

3.4.2 Opportunity Fit: finding new opportunities that fit your size.

3.5 Strength and Weakness: openings created by the strength of others.

3.7 Defining the Ground: redefining a competitive arena to create relative mismatches.

5.6 Defensive Advances: balancing defending and advancing positions.

5.6.1 Defense Priority: why defense has first claim on our resources.

9.4 Crisis Defense: how vulnerabilities are exploited and defended during a crisis.

9.4.1 Division Defense: preventing organizational division during a crisis.

9.4.2 Panic Defense: the mistakes arising from panic during a crisis.

9.4.3 Defending Openings: how to defend openings created by a crisis.

9.4.4 Defending Alliances: dealing with guilt by association.

9.4.5 Defensive Balance: using short-term conditions to tip the balance in a crisis.

Chapter 5

Momentum – Intense Intimacy

Once you have found a close relationship, you need to build and maintain intensity. Sex can be casual, but rel intimacy is always powerful. Intensity is created from what Sun Tzu calls *momentum*. Momentum isn't created by simply doing what you have done well in the past. Sun Tzu's science of strategy teaches that momentum comes from first establishing a set of expectations and then creating excitement by exceeding those expectations.

Surprise, innovation, and creativity are a key ideas in building this intensity, but it takes more than just tricks. Unless you first satisfy people's expectations for normal behavior, surprise is worse than useless. It is disconcerting and even scary.

Sun Tzu's concept of innovation starts by relying on consistency. People need a degree of predictability. They want their expectations to be satisfied. Without first establishing a baseline of consistency, innovation and surprise just create chaos and confusion.

Once you meet a set of relationship expectations, you then have an infinite number of ways to create intensity through surprise and innovation. Sun Tzu offers a simple formula for coming up with a continual flow of possible surprises.

Together, the shift between meeting expectations and exceeding them creates momentum, intensity, and the feeling of true intimacy, but timing is also important to get the most out this process. Momentum builds up pressure while timing releases that pressure at the right instant to create intimacy. Timing introduces a critical amount of control into the chaos of everyday living.

The Art of War: Momentum

STANDARDS:

Momentum requires developing a set of standards that customers can depend upon.

SUN TZU SAID:

You control a large group the same as you control a few. 1
You just divide their ranks correctly.
You fight a large army the same as you fight a small one.
You only need the right position and communication.
You may meet a large enemy army.
You must be able to sustain an enemy attack without being defeated.
You must correctly use both surprise and direct action.
Your army's position must increase your strength.
Troops flanking an enemy can smash them like eggs.
You must correctly use both strength and weakness.

It is the same in all battles. 2
You use a direct approach to engage the enemy.
You use surprise to win.

⁴You must use surprise for a successful invasion.
Surprise is as infinite as the weather and land.
Surprise is as inexhaustible as the flow of a river.

The Art of Love: **Intense Intimacy**

A LOVE SEEKER HEARS:

1 We must honor big commitments as well as small ones.
We must put a high priority on our shared moments.
Winning intimacy is the same as winning a kiss.
We need the right place and time.
We may have serious reservations.
We can conquer our doubts without destroying the relationship.
We need to be both exciting and comfortable.
Our closeness must increase our appeal.
New passion can easily overcome any resistance.
We must leverage both our strengths and weaknesses.

2 It is the same in any romance.
We must be dependable to build a relationship.
We must be exciting to create passion.

We must be inventive to maintain lasting love.
We can offer an infinite number of new experiences.
Use surprise to keep the relationship moving forward.

INNOVATION:

All relationships are the same and all are unique. Start with what is familiar, but win using creativity.

The Art of War: **Momentum**

⁷You can be stopped and yet recover the initiative.
You must use your days and months correctly.

⁹If you are defeated, you can recover.
You must use the four seasons correctly.

¹¹There are only a few notes in the scale.
Yet you can always rearrange them.
You can never hear every song of victory.

¹⁴There are only a few basic colors.
Yet you can always mix them.
You can never see all the shades of victory.

¹⁷There are only a few flavors.
Yet you can always blend them.
You can never taste all the flavors of victory.

²⁰You fight with momentum.
There are only a few types of surprises and direct actions.
Yet you can always vary the ones you use.
There is no limit to the ways you can win.

²⁴Surprise and direct action give birth to each other.
They are like a circle without end.
You cannot exhaust all their possible combinations!

Surging waters flow together rapidly. 3
Its pressure washes away boulders.
This is momentum.

The Art of Love: **Intense Intimacy**

A relationship can lose its spark and then be revived.
We must use our time together well.

We can make mistakes and still recover.
We must give the relationship time to grow.

There are only a few words of affection.
But we can always rearrange them.
There is no limit to ways we can voice our love.

There are only a few signs of affection.
Yet, we can always mingle them.
There is no limit to the ways we can show our love.

There are only a few forms of lovemaking.
Yet, we can always combine them.
We will never run out of expressions of our love.

We win love with intimacy.
There are only a few ways to create excitement and trust.
Yet, we can vary the ones we use.
There is no limit to the ways we can keep love passionate.

Excitement and trust give birth to each other.
Excitement is only stimulating if we are reliable.
Using both, we will never lose our lover's interest.

3 Passion brings people together rapidly.
It changes everything in our lives.
This is intimacy.

The Art of War: **Momentum**

⁴A hawk suddenly strikes a bird.
Its contact alone kills the prey.
This is timing.

⁷You must fight only winning battles.
Your momentum must be overwhelming.
Your timing must be exact.

¹⁰Your momentum is like the tension of a bent crossbow.
Your timing is like the pulling of a trigger.

War is very complicated and confusing.
Battle is chaotic.
Nevertheless, you must not allow chaos.

⁴War is very sloppy and messy.
Positions turn around.
Nevertheless, you must never be defeated.

⁷Chaos gives birth to control.
Fear gives birth to courage.
Weakness gives birth to strength.

¹⁰You must control chaos.
This depends on your planning.
Your men must brave their fears.
This depends on momentum.

¹⁴You have strengths and weaknesses.
These come from your position.

MOMENTUM:

Dependable standards and constant improvement create pressure in the marketplace to buy.

The Art of Love: Intense Intimacy

We suddenly recognize our feelings.
Our awareness shatters our illusions.
This is commitment.

We want to win only lasting love.
Our passion must be overwhelming.
Our commitment must be real.

Intimacy in a relationship creates tension.
Commitment releases that tension.

4 Love is always complicated and confusing.
Relationships are chaotic.
Nevertheless, we must minimize conflict.

Love is sloppy and messy.
Roles are constantly changing.
Nevertheless, we must keep love alive.

Turmoil gives rise to stability.
Fear gives rise to trust.
Need gives rise to fervor.

We must control the craziness.
This depends on our foresight.
We must learn to trust completely.
This requires intimacy.

We all have strengths and weaknesses.
We learn them from spending time together.

> **TIMING:**
>
> *Being dependable requires offering surprises, thereby winning attention and changing perceptions.*

The Art of War: **Momentum**

¹⁶You must force the enemy to move to your advantage.
Use your position.
The enemy must follow you.
Surrender a position.
The enemy must take it.
You can offer an advantage to move him.
You can use your men to move him.
You can use your strength to hold him.

You want a successful battle. 5
To do this, you must seek momentum.
Do not just demand a good fight from your people.
You must pick good people and then give them momentum.

⁵You must create momentum.
You create it with your men during battle.
This is comparable to rolling trees and stones.
Trees and stones roll because of their shape and weight.
Offer men safety and they will stay calm.
Endanger them and they will act.
Give them a place and they will hold.
Round them up and they will march.

¹³You make your men powerful in battle with momentum.
This should be like rolling round stones down over a high, steep cliff.
Momentum is critical.

The Art of Love: **Intense Intimacy**

We want our relationship to get better with time.
Use your partnership.
Our romantic partner must follow us.
Be willing to make a commitment.
Your romantic partner must accept it.
We can create an opportunity for intimacy.
We can use our actions to invite intimacy.
We can use our passion to hold the relationship together.

5 We want our relationship to be satisfying.
To do this, we must seek intimacy.
Do not expect to be loved simply for your good qualities.
Pick the right person and then become intimate.

We must create intimacy.
We create it using our skill within the relationship.
Men and women are naturally attracted.
Attraction arises from both our similarities and differences.
When we offer friendship, our partner relaxes.
When we use sex, our partner reacts.
Offer your beloved stability to hold them.
Offer your beloved excitement to move them.

We make ourselves more lovable by creating intimacy.
This is simply leveraging the natural power of
sexual attraction.
Use intimacy.

Related Articles from *Sun Tzu's Playbook*

In his fifth chapter, Sun Tzu explains the process for creating momentum. To learn the step-by-step techniques involved, we recommend the Sun Tzu's Art of War Playbook articles listed below.

1.2 Subobjective Positions: the subjective and objective aspects of a position.

7.0 Creating Momentum: how momentum requires creativity.

7.1 Order from Chaos: the value of chaos in creating competitive momentum.

7.1.1 Creating Surprise: creating surprise using our chaotic environment.

7.1.2 Momentum Psychology: the psychology of surprise.

7.1.3 Standards and Innovation: the methodology of creativity.

7.2 Standards First: the role of standards in creating connections with others.

7.2.1 Proven Methods: identifying and recognizing the limits of best practices.

7.2.2 Preparing Expectations: how we shape other people's expectations.

7.3 Strategic Innovation: a simple system for innovation.

7.3.1 Expected Elements: dividing processes and systems into components.

7.3.2 Elemental Rearrangement: seeing invention as rearranging proven elements.

7.3.3 Creative Innovation: the more advanced methods for innovation.

7.4 Competitive Timing: the role of timing in creating momentum.

7.4.1 Timing Methods: the three simplest methods of controlling timing.

7.4.2 Momentum Timing: the relative value of momentum at various times in a campaign.

7.4.3 Interrupting Patterns: how repetition creates patterns for surprise.

7.5 Momentum Limitations: the implications of momentum's temporary nature.

7.5.1 Momentum Conversion: converting momentum into positions with more value.

7.5.2 The Spread of Innovation: the spread of innovation to advance our position.

7.6 Productive Competition: using momentum to produce more resources.

7.6.1 Resource Discovery: using innovation to create value from seemingly worthless resources.

7.6.2 Ground Creation: the creation of new competitive ground to be successful.

Chapter 6

Weakness and Strength — Needs and Satisfaction

Sun Tzu teaches you not to try to force your way forward. Instead, you look for openings that make progress easy. To see openings, you need to understand two opposing but complementary concepts. The first concept is "weakness," but it also means needs, emptiness, and a lack of resources. The second concept is "strength," but it also means satisfaction, fullness, and a surplus of resources. Together these two ideas describe a cycle that creates and fills openings naturally.

The two sexes are complementary opposites, with different abilities and desires. Those who are not self-centered do not look for more of what they already have but for what they lack. You have probably heard that nature abhors a vacuum. This is true in the relationships as well. Compatibility does not mean being identical. It means being complementary. Weak, empty, and needy conditions cry out to be satisfied. In Sun Tzu's system, these weakness states are considered "openings" that determine our opportunities.

However, a powerful psychological force prevents people from seeing these opportunities. People see weakness and neediness as problems not opportunities. They are frightened by neediness in themselves and others. The courageous embrace weakness and emptiness. By doing so, you become strong.

However, fullness and satisfaction are only temporary states. They naturally revert to back to emptiness and neediness over time. The challenge of meeting each others' needs never ends.

The Art of War: Weakness and Strength

SUN TZU SAID:

Always arrive first to the empty battlefield to await the 1 enemy at your leisure.
After the battleground is occupied and you hurry to it, fighting is more difficult.

³You want a successful battle.
Move your men, but not into opposing forces.

⁵You can make the enemy come to you.
Offer him an advantage.
You can make the enemy avoid coming to you.
Threaten him with danger.

⁹When the enemy is fresh, you can tire him.
When he is well fed, you can starve him.
When he is relaxed, you can move him.

WEAKNESS:

Competitors' weaknesses arise naturally from unsatisfied customer needs. Needs create opportunities.

The Art of Love: **Needs and Satisfaction**

A LOVE SEEKER HEARS:

1 We want the advantage of a romance with a person who needs us.
Avoid pursing a person who is happy without a relationship.

We want a solid romantic relationship.
Do not romance someone who fights against relationships.

We can entice someone that we would like to chase after us.
We must make ourselves attractive.
We can avoid relationships that we don't want.
We can make it unpleasant to be around us.

When someone is rested, we can tire them.
When someone is satisfied, we can entice them.
When someone is relaxed, we can get them excited.

STRENGTHS:

Every person has areas of strength that make some things easier for them than others.

The Art of War: **Weakness and Strength**

Leave any place without haste. **2**
Hurry to where you are unexpected.
You can easily march hundreds of miles without tiring.
To do so, travel through areas that are deserted.
You must take whatever you attack.
Attack when there is no defense.
You must have walls to defend.
Defend where it is impossible to attack.

> AVOIDANCE:
>
> *Success depends upon avoiding competitive challenges while you move to develop better positions.*

⁹Be skilled in attacking.
Give the enemy no idea where to defend.

¹¹Be skillful in your defense.
Give the enemy no idea where to attack.

Be subtle! Be subtle! **3**
Arrive without any clear formation.
Ghostly! Ghostly!
Arrive without a sound.
You must use all your skill to control the enemy's decisions.

⁶Advance where he can't defend.
Charge through his openings.
Withdraw where the enemy cannot chase you.
Move quickly so that he cannot catch you.

¹⁰Always pick your own battles.

The Art of Love: **Needs and Satisfaction**

2. Never abandon a relationship too quickly.
Avoid all the predictable moves.
People can go through a lot without tiring of each other.
To stay together, they must need one another.
Develop a relationship that must succeed.
Find a partner who needs you.
Defend yourself from heartbreak.
Build a relationship that is solid.

Be skilled in winning love.
Keep your insecurities to yourself.

Be skilled in keeping love.
Give your partner no reason to be insecure.

3. Keep your doubts to yourself.
Build a relationship without demanding more.
Avoid being critical.
Let the relationship develop quietly.
You must skillfully control your partner's perceptions.

We can get closer without making our partners defensive.
We can fill the holes in their lives.
We can pull back from those who don't satisfy us.
We can do it quickly before commitment develops.

We must choose the right relationship.

> **SPECIALIZE:**
>
> *Focus your talents on areas on the relationship that are difficult for rivals to duplicate.*

The Art of War: Weakness and Strength

The enemy can hide behind high walls and deep trenches.
Do not try to win by fighting him directly.
Instead, attack a place that he must recapture.
Avoid the battles that you don't want.
You can divide the ground and yet defend it.
Don't give the enemy anything to win.
Divert him by coming to where you defend.

4
Make other men take a position while you take none.
Then focus your forces where the enemy divides his forces.
Where you focus, you unite your forces.
When the enemy divides, he creates many small groups.
You want your large group to attack one of his small ones.
Then you have many men where the enemy has but a few.
Your larger force can overwhelm his smaller one.
Then go on to the next small enemy group.
You can take them one at a time.

5
You must keep the place that you have chosen as a battleground a secret.
The enemy must not know.
Force the enemy to prepare his defense in many places.
You want the enemy to defend many places.
Then you can choose where to fight.
His forces will be weak there.

SECRECY:

You cannot exploit the weakness of your opponents if everyone knows what you are doing.

The Art of Love: Needs and Satisfaction

The right partner can be hard to find and attract.
We should not initially pursue anyone specifically.
Instead, we put ourselves where we can meet good people.
We can avoid the wrong relationship.
We separate ourselves from fools for self-protection.
Don't give idiots a reason to pursue you.
Distract losers from getting to know you.

4 Let others express their feelings before you voice yours.
Bestow your affections on a person who needs love.
Focus your attention on the person you are with.
Let others divide their attentions among many people.
Don't try to juggle many relationships at once.
Spend time with someone who spends little time elsewhere.
You can easily make progress in this relationship.
If one person isn't right, you can move on.
You capture hearts one at a time.

5 We must keep our potential interest in someone new a secret.
No one must suspect it.
Let others defend themselves from serious relationships.
Let others try to be appear perfect in every way so that they can win affection.
We can choose when to fight for attention.
They will have a moment of weakness.
Competition will be weak there.

ADAPTABILITY:

Romance is not the execution of some grand plan but constantly adjusting to needs of the situation.

The Art of War: **Weakness and Strength**

⁷If he reinforces his front lines, he depletes his rear.
If he reinforces his rear, he depletes his front.
If he reinforces his right flank, he depletes his left.
If he reinforces his left flank, he depletes his right.
Without knowing the place of attack, he cannot prepare.
Without knowing the right place, he will be weak everywhere.

> **WEAK POINTS:**
>
> *You must see a competitor's most serious weak points and focus your strengths on exploiting them.*

¹³The enemy has weak points.
Prepare your men against them.
He has strong points.
Make his men prepare themselves against you.

You must know the battleground. **6**
You must know the time of battle.
You can then travel a thousand miles and still win the battle.

⁴The enemy should not know the battleground.
He shouldn't know the time of battle.
His left flank will be unable to support his right.
His right will be unable to support his left.
His front lines will be unable to support his rear.
His rear will be unable to support his front.
His support is distant even if it is only ten miles away.
What unknown place can be close?

¹²You control the balance of forces.
The enemy may have many men but they are superfluous.
How can they help him to victory?

The Art of Love: **Needs and Satisfaction**

Some people pit visible relationships against secret ones.
In looking for backup relationships, they weaken current ones.
When they have on kind of relationship, they want another kind.
When they get what they think they wanted, they don't want it..
Without knowing what they are looking for, they focus
only on the hunt.
Without looking for the best relationship, none of their
relationships can work.

Everyone has needs.
Prepare yourself to address them.
Everyone has something to offer.
Know what you need in a relationship.

6 You must recognize a potential partner.
You must know when a connection will work.
You can then avoid rejection and build a relationship.

Unsuccessful lovers don't recognize potential partners.
They are unaware of how they are wasting their time.
They learn nothing from one relationship to help the next.
They are unable to discover a single person to care about.
They date the wrong people and ignore the better ones.
They judge people by appearance and forget character.
They miss the potential partner in front of them.
What stranger can they get close to?

Our behavior determines our relationships.
A person can have many suitors but they are superfluous.
How can meaningless contacts help us find love?

> NEEDS:
>
> *Everyone has an infinite number of needs. You must choose those that you can best address.*

The Art of War: **Weakness and Strength**

[15]We say:
You must let victory happen.

[17]The enemy may have many men.
You can still control him without a fight.

When you form your strategy, know the strengths and **7**
weaknesses of your plan.
When you execute a plan, know how to manage both action
and inaction.
When you take a position, know the deadly and the winning
grounds.
When you enter into battle, know when you have too many
or too few men.

[5]Use your position as your war's centerpiece.
Arrive at the battle without a formation.
Don't take a position in advance.
Then even the best spies can't report it.
Even the wisest general cannot plan to counter you.
Take a position where you can triumph using superior numbers.
Keep opposing forces ignorant.
Everyone should learn your location after your position has
given you success.
No one should know how your location gives you a winning
position.
Make a successful battle one from which the enemy cannot
recover.
You must continually adjust your position to his position.

The Art of Love: **Needs and Satisfaction**

The truth is simple.
We must let love happen.

There are many people in the world.
We can find the right partner without worrying.

7 When you get serious about a relationship, know your personal strengths and weaknesses.
When meeting people, you must know when to talk and when to listen.
When sharing experiences, know who is worth your time and who isn't.
When forming a relationship, know when you are giving too much or too little.

Use friendship as the basis for finding love.
Meet people without prejudging them.
Avoid premature intimacies.
Then even the worst gossips cannot speak badly of you.
Then even the most protective person cannot misjudge you.
In groups, work at knowing more individuals than anyone else.
Keep your romantic interests a secret.
The object of your affection should learn your feelings only when your relationship is solid.
Your partner should not worry about where the relationship is headed.
When compared to others within your group, you want to stand out in a memorable way.
You continually weigh your feelings against your intendeds.

The Art of War: **Weakness and Strength**

Manage your military position like water. **8**
Water takes every shape.
It avoids the high and moves to the low.
Your war can take any shape.
It must avoid the strong and strike the weak.
Water follows the shape of the land that directs its flow.
Your forces follow the enemy, who determines how you win.

[8]Make war without a standard approach.
Water has no consistent shape.
If you follow the enemy's shifts and changes, you can always find a way to win.
We call this shadowing.

[12]Fight five different campaigns without a firm rule for victory.
Use all four seasons without a consistent position.
Your timing must be sudden.
A few weeks determine your failure or success.

ADJUSTMENT:

Continuously adjust to continuous change.

The Art of Love: **Needs and Satisfaction**

8 You must be flexible in a romantic relationship.
There are many roles.
Avoid high expectations and demand little.
Romance can take many forms.
Use your strengths to compliment another's needs.
Let the needs of your partner dictate your actions.
How well you complete each other decides your future.

Avoid repeating the same mistakes in your relationship.
You don't always have to play the same role.
If you always embrace the changes in your partner's life, you can always win love.
This is called shadowing.

In any relationship, be open to new possibilities.
Use current opportunities to create new shared experiences.
Commitments can come quickly.
A few weeks can determine your whole future.

URGENCY:

You satisfy your needs by satisfying another's needs.

Related Articles from *Sun Tzu's Playbook*

In chapter six, Sun Tzu explains how to find opportunities by leveraging opposites. To learn the step-by-step techniques involved, we recommend the Sun Tzu's Art of War Playbook *articles listed below.*

1.2.1 Competitive Landscapes: the arenas in which rivals jockey for position.

1.2.2 Exploiting Exploration: how competitive landscapes are searched and positions utilized.

1.2.3 Position Complexity: how strategic positions arise from interactions in complex environments.

1.3.1 Competitive Comparison: competition as the comparison of positions.

2.4 Contact Networks: the range of contacts needed to create perspective.

2.4.1 Ground Perspective: getting information on a new competitive arena.

2.4.2 Climate Perspective: getting perspective on temporary external conditions.

2.4.3 Command Perspective: developing sources for understanding decision-makers.

2.4.4 Methods Perspective: developing contacts who understand best practices.

2.4.5 Mission Perspective: how we develop and use a perspective on motivation.

2.5 The Big Picture: building big-picture strategic awareness.

2.6 Knowledge Leverage: getting competitive value out of knowledge.

2.7 Information Secrecy: the role of limiting information in controlling relationships.

3.2.3 Complementary Opposites: the dynamics of balance from opposing forces.

3.2.4 Emptiness and Fullness: rules on the transformations between emptiness and fullness.

3.2.5 Dynamic Reversal: how situations reverse themselves naturally.

3.5 Strength and Weakness: six rules regarding openings created by the strength of others.

3.6 Leveraging Subjectivity: openings between subjective and objective positions.

3.7 Defining the Ground: redefining a competitive arena to create relative mismatches.

3.8 Strategic Matrix Analysis: two-dimensional representations of strategic space.

4.7 Competitive Weakness: how certain opportunities can bring out our weaknesses.

4.7.1 Command Weaknesses: the character flaws of leaders and how to exploit them.

4.7.2 Group Weaknesses: organizational weakness and where groups fail.

6.7 Tailoring to Conditions: overcoming opposition using conditions in the environment.

6.7.1 Form Adjustments: adapting responses based on the form of the ground.

6.7.2 Size Adjustments: adapting responses based on comparing size of forces.

6.7.3 Strength Adjustments: adapting responses based on unity of opposing forces.

6.8 Competitive Psychology: improving competitive psychology even in adversity and failure.

6.8.1 Adversity and Creativity: how we use adversity to spark our creativity.

6.8.2 Strength in Adversity: using adversity to increase a group's unity and focus.

Chapter 7

Armed Conflict – Relationship Friction

Friction in a relationship is impossible to avoid. Even the most successful partners feel friction now and again. The closer you become, the more potential you create for a contest of wills. Sun Tzu's system is designed to avoid as much conflict as possible. However, in the end, to survive, you must deal conflict when it arises.

All successful relationships focus on building up common ground not on bumping heads. Sun Tzu teaches us to avoid unnecessary battles. Even if you "win" these internal battles, getting your own way, your relationship will suffer for it. Winning these internal conflicts can destroy your chances of happiness. The secret of avoiding conflict and, when necessary, dealing with confrontations, is commnuication that controls another's perceptions.

You must respect your partner's opinions. You listen to them. You must avoid frustrating their desires. You inspire them to make commitments to you. You must both claim and share the credit for accomplishments.

Communication is the key to handling the fiction that arises. You have to speak in a way that allows others to hear you. You have to pick the right time and place to resolve issues. There are a number of specific mistakes that most people make during confrontations that you must learn how to avoid.

The Art of War: Armed Conflict

SUN TZU SAID:

Everyone uses the arts of war. 1
You accept orders from the government.
Then you assemble your army.
You organize your men and build camps.
You must avoid disasters from armed conflict.

[6]Seeking armed conflict can be disastrous.
Because of this, a detour can be the shortest path.
Because of this, problems can become opportunities.

CONFLICT:

Strategy teaches that conflict is always costly so it is ideally avoided whenever possible.

[9]Use an indirect route as your highway.
Use the search for advantage to guide you.
When you fall behind, you must catch up.
When you get ahead, you must wait.
You must know the detour that most directly accomplishes your plan.

[14]Undertake armed conflict when you have an advantage.
Seeking armed conflict for its own sake is dangerous.

The Art of Love: **Relationship Friction**

A LOVE SEEKER HEARS:

1 Everyone wants to find true love.
We get our expectations from our family.
Over time we develop our character.
We find a potential partner and build a relationship.
We must then avoid problems from a contest of wills.

Conflict is costly to any relationship.
Because of this, we must be willing to compromise.
We must turn potential conflicts into opportunities.

You must go out of your way to avoid a contest of wills.
Let your search for common goals guide you.
If you fall behind in the relationship, you must catch up.
If you are moving too fast, you must wait.
You must find an indirect way to get what you need to win love.

CONTACT:

The difference between success and failure is how well we handle our contact with others..

You may sometimes quarrel and form a closer bond afterward.
But looking for a quarrel for selfish reasons is just foolish.

The Art of War: **Armed Conflict**

You can build up an army to fight for an advantage. 2
Then you won't catch the enemy.
You can force your army to go fight for an advantage.
Then you abandon your heavy supply wagons.

⁵You keep only your armor and hurry after the enemy.
You avoid stopping day or night.
You use many roads at the same time.
You go hundreds of miles to fight for an advantage.
Then the enemy catches your commanders and your army.
Your strong soldiers get there first.
Your weaker soldiers follow behind.
Using this approach, only one in ten will arrive.
You can try to go fifty miles to fight for an advantage.
Then your commanders and army will stumble.
Using this method, only half of your soldiers will make it.
You can try to go thirty miles to fight for an advantage.
Then only two out of three get there.

FIGHTING:

You do not create opportunities by fighting for them. The use of force without strategy is wasted effort.

¹⁸If you make your army travel without good
supply lines, your army will die.
Without supplies and food, your army will die.
If you don't save the harvest, your army will die.

The Art of Love: **Relationship Friction**

2 You think you can start a fight to force a commitment.
Then you make yourself look selfish.
You can get caught up with the idea of winning the battle.
You forget you are seeking a relationship that can last.

You can try to defend yourself and prove your lover wrong.
You can go on arguing forever.
You can try many different tactics.
You can do everything imaginable to prove you are right.
But your lover ignores your logic and sincerity.
Your best arguments only hurt your lover's feelings.
Your weakest arguments make you look foolish.
Ninety percent of the time, such arguments are destructive.
You can use arguments to express your frustrations.
You will then make yourself look weak.
Half the time you will not be understood.
You can use arguments to test the relationship.
It will cost you more than it is worth.

If you try to win affection without deep emotional bonds, you will fail.
Without trust and self-sacrifice, you will fail.
If you don't cultivate companionship, you will fail.

> **RESOURCES:**
> *Resources used to tear down others are wasted. Resources used to build up our knowledge of others will win.*

[21]Do not let any of your potential enemies know what you are planning.
Still, you must not hesitate to form alliances.
You must know the mountains and forests.
You must know where the obstructions are.
You must know where the marshes are.
If you don't, you cannot move the army.
If you don't, you must use local guides.
If you don't, you can't take advantage of the terrain.

3 You make war using a deceptive position.
If you use deception, then you can move.
Using deception, you can upset the enemy and change the situation.
You can move as quickly as the wind.
You can rise like the forest.
You can invade and plunder like fire.
You can stay as motionless as a mountain.
You can be as mysterious as the fog.
You can strike like sounding thunder.

DECEPTION:

Success comes from controlling people's perceptions by shaping the way situations must appear to them.

[10]Divide your troops to plunder the villages.
When on open ground, dividing is an advantage.
Don't worry about organization; just move.
Be the first to find a new route that leads directly to a winning plan.
This is how you are successful at armed conflict.

The Art of Love: Relationship Friction

Instead, you must keep quiet about your desire for a closer relationship.
You must bond with your partner.
You must know how your partner thinks.
You must know where the potential problems lie.
You must know where uncertainties will arise.
If you don't, the relationship won't blossom.
You must know your partner's friends.
If you don't, they cannot help you with the relationship.

3 You must hide your ultimate hopes and fears.
Without expectations, a relationship is free to grow.
Without expectations, you can upset your partner and shift the relationship.
You must sometimes adapt quickly.
You must sometimes take a stand.
You must sometimes move aggressively.
You must sometimes do nothing.
You must sometimes keep an air of mystery.
You must sometimes stand out from the crowd.

Divide your time among different groups of people.
In searching for connection, spreading out is works.
Don't worry about the future; just make contacts.
Move quickly to find a creative path to meeting more compatible people.
This is how you avoid contests of will.

> **PERCEPTION:**
>
> *We can only know each other through our perceptions so we must manage what others perceive.*

The Art of War: **Armed Conflict**

Military experience says: 4
"You can speak, but you will not be heard.
You must use gongs and drums.
You cannot really see your forces just by looking.
You must use banners and flags."

⁶You must master gongs, drums, banners, and flags.
Place people as a single unit where they can all see and hear.
You must unite them as one.
Then the brave cannot advance alone.
The fearful cannot withdraw alone.
You must force them to act as a group.

¹²In night battles, you must use numerous fires and drums.
In day battles, you must use many banners and flags.
You must position your people to control what they see and hear.

You control your army by controlling its morale. 5
As a general, you must be able to control emotions.

³In the morning, a person's energy is high.
During the day, it fades.
By evening, a person's thoughts turn to home.
You must use your troops wisely.
Avoid the enemy's high spirits.
Strike when his men are lazy and want to go home.
This is how you master energy.

The Art of Love: **Relationship Friction**

4 Experience in love teaches us:
We can talk, but we won't be understood.
We must illustrate our feelings.
We never know where we stand just by looking.
We must learn to interpret signals.

Use examples, humor, signals, and signs.
Put yourself in a position where you are understood clearly.
You must have a single, clear message.
Do not let your strengths obscure your needs.
Do not let your needs disguise your strength.
Let your partner experience you as a complete person.

If we are quiet, we must work harder to be heard.
If we are loud, we must learn more subtle signals
We must be sensitive to how well other people see and hear us.

5 You control your image by considering people's feelings.
You must be able to control your own emotions.

Early in the day, people are energetic.
During the day, their energy fades.
In the evening, people's thoughts turn to home.
We must time any criticism correctly.
Avoid exciting defensiveness.
Bring up problems when their defenses are down.
This is how you control energy.

The Art of War: **Armed Conflict**

¹⁰Use discipline to await the chaos of battle.
Keep relaxed to await a crisis.
This is how you master emotion.

¹³Stay close to home to await a distant enemy.
Stay comfortable to await the weary enemy.
Stay well fed to await the hungry enemy.
This is how you master power.

Don't entice the enemy when his ranks are orderly. 6
You must not attack when his formations are solid.
This is how you master adaptation.

⁴You must follow these military rules.
Do not take a position facing the high ground.
Do not oppose those with their backs to the wall.
Do not follow those who pretend to flee.
Do not attack the enemy's strongest men.
Do not swallow the enemy's bait.
Do not block an army that is heading home.
Leave an escape outlet for a surrounded army.
Do not press a desperate foe.
This is how you use military skills.

EMOTION:

Strategy teaches that emotion is the key to action. If you control emotions, you control actions.

The Art of Love: **Relationship Friction**

Keep calm when inevitable conflicts arise.
Laugh at yourself in a crisis.
This is how you master your own emotions.

Stay close to home to await a distant partner.
Stay well-rested to await a weary partner.
Stay satisfied to await a needy partner.
This is how you master influence.

6 Do not enter into a contest of wills to test another's love.
You must not criticize your beloved out of insecurity.
This is how you master adapting.

You must follow these rules in romance:
Do not defend yourself when you are wrong.
Do not force someone to defend him or herself.
Do not chase someone who pretends to avoid you.
Do not criticize your partner's strongest traits.
Do not believe everything you hear.
Do not block a partner from showing affection.
Leave your partner a way to save face.
Do not make demands and threats.
This is the art of love.

MESSAGE:

Your message to others must not be how great you are, but how great you can make them feel.

Related Articles from *Sun Tzu's Playbook*

In chapter seven, Sun Tzu teaches us to focus on building positions instead of on tearing down opponents. To learn the step-by-step techniques involved, we recommend the Sun Tzu's Art of War Playbook *articles listed below.*

1.2.1 Competitive Landscapes: the arenas in which rivals jockey for position.

1.3.1 Competitive Comparison: competition as the comparison of positions.

1.5 Competing Agents: characteristics of competitors.

1.7 Competitive Power: the sources of superiority in challenges.

1.8.1 Creation and Destruction: the creation and destruction of competitive positions.

1.9 Competition and Production: the two opposing skill sets of competition and production.

2.1.3 Strategic Deception: misinformation and disinformation in competition.

2.6 Knowledge Leverage: getting competitive value out of knowledge.

2.7 Information Secrecy: the role of secrecy in relationships.

3.1 Strategic Economics: balancing the cost and benefits of positioning.

3.1.1 Resource Limitations: the inherent limitation of strategic resources.

3.1.3 Conflict Cost: the costly nature of resolving competitive comparisons by conflict.

3.1.6 Time Limitations: understanding the time limits on opportunities.

3.7 Defining the Ground: redefining a competitive arena to create relative mismatches.

4.7 Competitive Weakness: how certain opportunities can bring out our weaknesses.

6.1.2 Prioritizing Conditions: parsing complex competitive conditions into simple responses.

6.8 Competitive Psychology: improving competitive psychology even in adversity and failure.

7.4 Competitive Timing: the role of timing in creating momentum.

7.6 Productive Competition: using momentum to produce more resources.

7.6.2 Ground Creation: the creation of new competitive ground to be successful.

8.5 Leveraging Emotions: how we use emotion to obtain rewards.

9.5.2 Avoiding Emotion: the danger of exploiting environmental vulnerabilities for purely emotion reasons.

Chapter 8

Adaptability – Personal Flexibility

This chapter introduces the second part of Sun Tzu's book. Thus far, we have dealt with the basic principles of making good choices in relationships. This next section covers the rules for responding appropriately to changing situations. Remember, relationships are dynamic. Successful relationships must adjust to changing needs.

The next three chapters after this one cover long lists of specific situations, how to recognize them, and how to respond to them. This chapter is meant as a general introduction to the concept of adaptability itself.

Sun Tzu's idea of adaptability is situation specific. Personal flexibility doesn't mean that any response to a situation might work. An appropriate response is one that best addresses the situation. As long as you respond appropriately, you can constantly adapt your approach without being inconsistent in your results.

If you understand the changing situations in a relationship better than your partner, you can actually use the dynamics of the changing situation to shape behavior. People are unpredictable. If you want to improve your relationship, you have to learn to use the specific situation at hand to shape perceptions and expectations.

Mistakes in responding to situations often arise from flaws in character. The five weaknesses of character result not from a lack of intelligence but usually from an excess of emotion. Incorrect responses to unexpected changes have a way of making matters worse.

The Art of War: Adaptability

SUN TZU SAID:

Everyone uses the arts of war. 1
As a general, you get your orders from the government.
You gather your troops.
On dangerous ground, you must not camp.
Where the roads intersect, you must join your allies.
When an area is cut off, you must not delay in it.
When you are surrounded, you must scheme.
In a life-or-death situation, you must fight.
There are roads that you must not take.
There are armies that you must not fight.
There are strongholds that you must not attack.
There are positions that you must not defend.
There are government commands that must not be obeyed.

ADAPTABILITY:

Adaptability doesn't mean doing what you want. It means knowing the appropriate response to the situation.

14Military leaders must be experts in knowing how to adapt to find an advantage.
This will teach you the use of war.

The Art of Love: Personal Flexibility

A LOVE SEEKER HEARS:

1 Everyone uses the arts of love.
We get our expectations from our family.
We develop our character.
In a difficult relationship, we must not become dependent
When families are involved, we must find supporters.
If a relationship is going nowhere, we must get out of it.
If we are trapped, we must be inventive.
When a relationship is at stake, we must fight for it.
There are paths we must not take.
There are battles that we must not fight.
There are beliefs that we must not attack.
There are points of view that we must not defend.
There are criticisms from our parents that we must ignore.

To be successful at winning love, we must know how to be accepting.
Acceptance teaches us the meaning of love.

RESILIENCE:

You become more resilient when you see that no occurrence is good or bad in itself. All that matters is your response.

The Art of War: **Adaptability**

[16]Some commanders are not good at making adjustments to find an advantage.
They can know the shape of the terrain.
Still, they cannot find an advantageous position.

[19]Some military commanders do not know how to adjust their methods.
They can find an advantageous position.
Still, they cannot use their men effectively.

2 You must be creative in your planning.
You must adapt to your opportunities and weaknesses.
You can use a variety of approaches and still have a consistent result.
You must adjust to a variety of problems and consistently solve them.

3 You can deter your potential enemy by using his weaknesses against him.
You can keep your potential enemy's army busy by giving it work to do.
You can rush your potential enemy by offering him an advantageous position.

PLANNING:

Planning does not mean creating a rigid to-do list, but constantly rethinking what the situation demands.

The Art of Love: **Personal Flexibility**

Some people are too inflexible to accept the different habits of others.
They can appreciate the strengths of others.
Still, they cannot build a comfortable relationship.

Some people are unable to adapt their lives to make room to shar them with others.
They can see how they should change.
Still, they cannot reshape their lives in a meaningful way.

2 We must be inspired in our foresight.
We must accept that all partners have shortcomings.
We can accept different roles and consistently be true to our character.
A romance can have a variety of problems, but we can consistently solve them.

3 We can avoid conflict by using people's needs to prevent it.
We can keep our partner interested by making them work for the relationship.
We can hasten a commitment by giving our partner a reason to decide now.

> CHANGE:
>
> *Smart romantic partners embrace change because change is the source of all new opportunities for progress.*

The Art of War: **Adaptability**

You must make use of war. **4**
Do not trust that the enemy isn't coming.
Trust your readiness to meet him.
Do not trust that the enemy won't attack.
Rely only on your ability to pick a place that the enemy can't attack.

You can exploit five different faults in a leader. **5**
If he is willing to die, you can kill him.
If he wants to survive, you can capture him.
He may have a quick temper.
You can then provoke him with insults.
If he has a delicate sense of honor, you can disgrace him.
If he loves his people, you can create problems for him.
In every situation, look for these five weaknesses.
They are common faults in commanders.
They always lead to military disaster.

[11]To overturn an army, you must kill its general.
To do this, you must use these five weaknesses.
You must always look for them.

PREPARATION:

The battlefield always favors those who are the most mentally prepared for things not going according to plan.

The Art of Love: Personal Flexibility

4 You must make use of your love.
Do not think that you will not encounter problems.
Trust in your readiness to address them.
Do not take any relationship for granted.
Instead, work to build a relationship that you can both depend upon.

5 We can have five faults as a lover.
If we see ourselves as unlovable, we will not be loved.
If others can control us, they can take advantage of us.
We may have a quick temper.
Others can then provoke us to anger.
If we are too sensitive, our feelings are hurt too easily.
If we are easily infatuated, we will have problems.
In every situation, look for these five weaknesses.
Look for these characteristics in potential partners.
Knowing them can help us avoid disaster.

To win lasting love, you must find a worthy partner.
You must recognize these five weakness.
You must always look for them.

FLAWS:

People naturally resist change, but we best adapt to it by avoiding the mistakes we made in the past.

Related Articles from *Sun Tzu's Playbook*

In chapter eight, Sun Tzu teaches us the need to constantly adapt to the situation. To learn the step-by-step techniques involved, we recommend the Sun Tzu's Art of War Playbook *articles listed below.*

1.8 Progress Cycle: the adaptive loop by which positions are advanced.

1.8.1 Creation and Destruction: the creation and destruction of competitive positions.

1.8.2 The Adaptive Loop: the continual reiteration of position analysis.

1.8.3 Cycle Time: the importance of speed in feedback and reaction.

1.8.4 Probabilistic Process: the role of chance in strategic processes and systems.

4.7.1 Command Weaknesses: the character flaws of leaders and how to exploit them.

5.2.1 Choosing Adaptability: choosing actions that allow us a maximum of future flexibility.

5.2.2 Campaign Methods: the use of campaigns and their methods.

5.2.3 Unplanned Steps: distinguishing campaign adjustments from steps in a plan.

5.3 Reaction Time: the use of speed in choosing actions.

5.3.1 Speed and Quickness: the use of pace within a dynamic environment.

6.0 Situation Response: selecting the actions most appropriate to a situation.

6.1 Situation Recognition: situation recognition in making advances.

6.1.1 Conditioned Reflexes: how we develop automatic, instantaneous responses.

6.1.2 Prioritizing Conditions: parsing complex competitive conditions into simple responses.

6.2 Campaign Evaluation: how we justify continued investment in an ongoing campaign.

6.2.1 Campaign Flow: seeing campaigns as a series of situations that flow logically from one to another.

6.2.2 Campaign Goals: assessing the value of a campaign by a larger mission.

6.3 Campaign Patterns: how knowing campaign stages gives us insight into our situation.

6.5 Nine Responses: the best responses to the nine common competitive situations.

6.7 Tailoring to Conditions: overcoming opposition using conditions in the environment.

6.7.1 Form Adjustments: adapting our responses based on the form of the ground.

6.7.2 Size Adjustments: adapting responses based on the relative size of opposing forces.

6.7.3 Strength Adjustments: how to adapt responses based on the relative strength of opposing missions.

Heaven

Ground

Chapter 9

Armed March — Love's Path

A committed relationship must weather to a variety of situations. As you move through your life, you are going to encounter new challenges that affects your relationship. This detailed chapter addresses how you must respond to the specific nature of those challenges. When it comes to making progress in a relationship, the devil is in the details. You must know how to recognize each specific situation and respond appropriately.

When moving down love's path, the first thing that you must take into consideration is the type of relationship you are in. Classical strategy describes four general type of "terrains" that affect your position. Some relationship are inequitable. Others are fast-changing. Some are uncertain. And a few are broad, stable, and solid. Each type has its own rules.

At any point of a relationship, you always want to control the high ground. This gets the forces shaping the situation on your side. Temporary and hidden dangers are inherent in exploring a relationship. You need to see what is happening in a relationship. This requires recognizing various signs in the relationship and interpret them correctly.

The most detailed lessons of this chapter deal with understanding the unspoken messages between people. You can only determine the conditions and intentions of others by interpreting their behavior. You have to recognize when you have gone as far as you can in a relationship and how you can regroup.

The Art of War: **Armed March**

SUN TZU SAID:

Anyone moving an army must adjust to the enemy. 1
When caught in the mountains, rely on their valleys.
Position yourself on the heights facing the sun.
To win your battles, never attack uphill.
This is how you position your army in the mountains.

⁶When water blocks you, keep far away from it.
Let the invader cross the river and wait for him.
Do not meet him in midstream.
Wait for him to get half his forces across and then
take advantage of the situation.

TERRAIN:

Strategy teaches that all terrains have a different form and these forms dictate how you must respond.

¹⁰You need to be able to fight.
You can't do that if you are caught in water when
you meet an invader.
Position yourself upstream, facing the sun.
Never face against the current.
Always position your army upstream when near
the water.

The Art of Love: **Love's Path**

A LOVE SEEKER HEARS:

1 In every relationship, we must adjust to our partner.
Avoid premature intimacy to keep a partner comfortable.
Hold to your ideals and be honest.
To win affection, never attack another's ideals.
This is how to get closer to real intimacy.

Avoid situations where life situations are changing.
When a partner is going through changes, be patient.
Do not try to force decisions during other changes.
Wait until the situation settles and know how to use recent changes.

We need to put in real effort.
We cannot get caught in the midst of changes when we meet the right person.
Look to the future, keeping your eyes open.
Never give into situation pressure.
This is how you get closer when dealing with changing situations.

PROGRESS:

As relationships progress, four common situations tend to arise. We must deal with them correctly.

The Art of War: **Armed March**

¹⁵You may have to move across marshes.
Move through them quickly without stopping.
You may meet the enemy in the middle of a marsh.
You must keep on the water grasses.
Keep your back to a clump of trees.
This is how you position your army in a marsh.

²¹On a level plateau, take a position that you can change.
Keep the higher ground on your right and to the rear.
Keep danger in front of you and safety behind.
This is how you position yourself on a level plateau.

²⁵You can find an advantage in all four of these situations.
Learn from the great emperor who used positioning to
conquer his four rivals.

2
Armies are stronger on high ground and weaker on low.
They are better camping on sunny southern hillsides than
on shady northern ones.
Provide for your army's health and place men correctly.
Your army will be free from disease.
Done correctly, this means victory.

⁶You must sometimes defend on a hill or riverbank.
You must keep on the south side in the sun.
Keep the uphill slope at your right rear.

⁹This will give the advantage to your army.
It will always give you a position of strength.

The Art of Love: **Love's Path**

You may not know where you stand in a relationship.
Take periods of uncertainty in stride.
You may feel insecure during periods of uncertainty.
You must stay well-grounded.
Protect your back.
This is how to get closer during periods of uncertainty.

In an equitable relationship, open yourself to change.
Keep your ideals at hand to support you.
Stay aware of problems and build trust.
This is how to get closer in an equitable relationship.

You can get closer in any situation.
Learn from successful relationships that can weather any type of problem.

2 Emotional relationships are stronger than physical ones.
We are stronger in an open, cheerful relationship than in a furtive, tortured one.
Keep your relationship healthy by sharing experiences.
Keep your relationship free from dishonesty.
Do this correctly, and you will find love.

Sometimes we must defend our principles under pressure.
We must stay optimistic and honest.
Keep in touch with your ideals.

This will make your relationship rewarding.
High standards always give you a position of strength.

The Art of War: **Armed March**

Stop the march when the rain swells the river into rapids. 3
You may want to ford the river.
Wait until it subsides.

⁴All regions can have seasonal mountain streams that can cut you off.
There are seasonal lakes.
There are seasonal blockages.
There are seasonal jungles.
There are seasonal floods.
There are seasonal fissures.
Get away from all these quickly.
Do not get close to them.
Keep them at a distance.
Maneuver the enemy close to them.
Position yourself facing these dangers.
Push the enemy back into them.

¹⁶Danger can hide on your army's flank.
There are reservoirs and lakes.
There are reeds and thickets.
There are mountain woods.
Their dense vegetation provides a hiding place.
You must cautiously search through them.
They can always hide an ambush.

SEASONS:

The changing climate part of every strategic position means that positions continually change.

The Art of Love: **Love's Path**

3 Slow the relationship down when it is moving too fast.
You may want to make a commitment.
Wait until obsession subsides.

All areas of a relationship run into recurring temporary changes
that create friction.
There are shifts in finances.
We have health problems.
We have family entanglements.
We get unexpected expenses.
We have temporary breakups
Get through these issues quickly.
Do not dwell on them.
Avoid wallowing in past problems.
Let others play with bad feelings
Face your problems directly.
Let others get mired in their problems.

Problems can hide in the shadows of our relationship.
Beware of secret histories.
Beware of furtive habits.
Beware of problems that are obvious to others.
Complex personalities can harbor problems.
We must get to know our lover well.
We don't want to be surprised.

> **PATIENCE:**
>
> *Unexpected changes endanger relationships only if we fail to realize what is happening.*

The Art of War: **Armed March**

Sometimes, the enemy is close by but remains calm. 4
Expect to find him in a natural stronghold.
Other times he remains at a distance but provokes battle.
He wants you to attack him.

⁵He sometimes shifts the position of his camp.
He is looking for an advantageous position.

⁷The trees in the forest move.
Expect that the enemy is coming.
The tall grasses obstruct your view.
Be suspicious.

¹¹The birds take flight.
Expect that the enemy is hiding.
Animals startle.
Expect an ambush.

¹⁵Notice the dust.
It sometimes rises high in a straight line.
Vehicles are coming.
The dust appears low in a wide band.
Foot soldiers are coming.
The dust seems scattered in different areas.
The enemy is collecting firewood.
Any dust is light and settling down.
The enemy is setting up camp.

COMPETITION:

Competition is part of the competitive environment and must be analyzed as part of that environment.

The Art of Love: **Love's Path**

4 A prospective lover is sometimes affectionate but quiet.
Expect that they are naturally self-confident.
Other times, they seem distant and angry.
They want you to show interest.

Sometimes a prospective lover makes a radical change.
They are trying to get your attention.

Certain routines begin to change.
Expect that a challenge is coming.
Discussions are like smoke screens.
Suspect something is up.

Mutual friends are nervous.
Expect your lover has a secret.
Others are jumpy.
Expect a surprise.

Notice the little things.
Sometimes clear signals point in the same direction.
A confrontation is coming.
Sometimes there are signs in a broad area.
Stubborn resistance is arising.
Sometimes there are hints only in certain areas.
Your lover is settling down.
You see fewer and fewer signs.
Your relationship is solid.

EVALUATION:

People don't always tell us what they are thinking, so we must judge them by how we see them acting.

The Art of War: **Armed March**

Your enemy speaks humbly while building up forces. 5
He is planning to advance.

³The enemy talks aggressively and pushes as if to advance.
He is planning to retreat.

⁵Small vehicles exit his camp first.
They move the army's flanks.
They are forming a battle line.

⁸Your enemy tries to sue for peace but without offering a treaty.
He is plotting.

¹⁰Your enemy's men run to leave and yet form ranks.
You should expect action.

¹²Half his army advances and the other half retreats.
He is luring you.

¹⁴Your enemy plans to fight but his men just stand there.
They are starving.

¹⁶Those who draw water drink it first.
They are thirsty.

¹⁸Your enemy sees an advantage but does not advance.
His men are tired.

The Art of Love: **Love's Path**

5 A conflict can seem unimportant but keeps growing.
It will get more serious.

You anticipate a potential conflict and prepare for it.
That problem will be minimal.

Sudden changes in the relationship aggravate problems that already exist.
You must address them.

Some conflicts seem to fade in the background but they remain unresolved.
They will arise again.

Some conflicts seem easily resolved but reappear later.
You need to do more.

Do not solve conflicts only to create new ones.
This is a trap.

Your lover has a reason to be angry but says nothing.
People have limits.

You always want to address your own issues first.
You are shortsighted.

You have an opportunity to get closer but do not take it.
You are tired.

The Art of War: **Armed March**

²⁰Birds gather.
Your enemy has abandoned his camp.

²²Your enemy's soldiers call in the night.
They are afraid.

²⁴Your enemy's army is raucous.
The men do not take their commander seriously.

²⁶Your enemy's banners and flags shift.
Order is breaking down.

²⁸Your enemy's officers are irritable.
They are exhausted.

JUDGMENT:

You best judge your competitors' situation by what they and their employees do rather than what they say.

³⁰Your enemy's men kill their horses for meat.
They are out of provisions.

³²They don't put their pots away or return to their tents.
They are desperate.

³⁴Enemy troops appear sincere and agreeable.
But their men are slow to speak to each other.
They are no longer united.

³⁷Your enemy offers too many incentives to his men.
He is in trouble.

The Art of Love: **Love's Path**

Gossips chatter.
Your lover has already moved on.

Your lover has difficulty sleeping at night
It is fear.

Your lover's friends are rude.
They don't take their friend's relationship seriously.

Your lover visibly signals a shift in allegiance.
A change is coming.

Your lover is suddenly short-tempered.
It is weariness.

Your lover starts selling valuable possessions.
Suspect money problems.

Your lover stops maintaining a separate apartment.
Expect a commitment.

You treat each other sincerely and agreeably.
Nevertheless, you no longer really talk.
You are no longer a team.

A lover offers too many incentives to spend time together.
This is insecurity.

> **PROBLEMS:**
>
> *In romance, we need to find the opportunities in the problems that our lover might be going through.*

The Art of War: **Armed March**

[39]Your enemy gives out too many punishments.
His men are weary.

[41]Your enemy first acts violently and then is afraid of your larger force.
His best troops have not arrived.

[43]Your enemy comes in a conciliatory manner.
He needs to rest and recuperate.

[45]Your enemy is angry and appears to welcome battle.
This goes on for a long time, but he doesn't attack.
He also doesn't leave the field.
You must watch him carefully.

If you are too weak to fight, you must find more men. **6**
In this situation, you must not act aggressively.
You must unite your forces.
Prepare for the enemy.
Recruit men and stay where you are.

[6]You must be cautious about making plans and adjust to the enemy.
You must gather more men.

EXPANSION:

Campaigns into new areas expand your control but they also spread your resources over a wider territory.

The Art of Love: **Love's Path**

A lover becomes suddenly too critical of you.
This shows limitations.

A lover first criticizes you and then seeks more affection from you.
Expect better from them.

A lover comes to you wanting to make up after a fight.
It is time to recover and relax.

A lover is angry and appears to want to fight.
This goes on for a long time without anything being said.
The tension doesn't go away.
You must pay attention to the situation.

6 When challenged, relationships need a reason to exist.
At that time, you must not demand commitment.
You must generate affection, expect problems, share experiences, and be patient.

You must plan carefully and work continually to build the relationship.
You must increase the bonds of trust between you.

PAUSING:

A relationship reaches its limit when our resources are stretched too thinly to contribute to it.

The Art of War: **Armed March**

With new, undedicated soldiers, you can depend on them ⁷
if you discipline them.
They will tend to disobey your orders.
If they do not obey your orders, they will be useless.

⁴You can depend on seasoned, dedicated soldiers.
But you must avoid disciplining them without reason.
Otherwise, you cannot use them.

⁷You must control your soldiers with esprit de corps.
You must bring them together by winning victories.
You must get them to believe in you.

¹⁰Make it easy for people to know what to do by training
your people.
Your people will then obey you.
If you do not make it easy for people to know what
to do, you won't train your people.
Then they will not obey.

¹⁴Make your commands easy to follow.
You must understand the way a crowd thinks.

YOUR TROOPS:

Your success depends totally on your ability to train, motivate, and manage the people with whom you work.

The Art of Love: **Love's Path**

7 You can depend on a new, untested relationship if you don't demand too much from it.
Otherwise, it will get confusing.
A confused relationship cannot move forward.

It is different with a long-term, established relationship.
You must avoid being too careful in it without reason.
If you always have to be careful, it is not working.

The two of you must develop the sense that you are a team.
You grow closer by sharing each other's successes.
You must trust in each other.

Make it easy to understand one another through honest communication.
You will then both know what to do.
If you do not take the time to talk, neither of you will be understood.
You will both make mistakes.

Start by understanding what you want.
You must then understand how your lover thinks.

REWARDS:

Our success depends on our ability to develop skills. Make it easy for others to support you.

Related Articles from *Sun Tzu's Playbook*

In chapter nine, Sun Tzu discusses the basics of recognizing conditions in new territory. To learn the step-by-step techniques involved, we recommend the Sun Tzu's Art of War Playbook *articles listed below.*

1.1.0 Position Paths: the continuity of strategic positions over time.

1.2.2 Exploiting Exploration: how competitive landscapes are searched and positions utilized.

2.1 Information Value: knowledge and communication as the basis of strategy.

2.1.1 Information Limits: making good decisions with limited information.

2.2.1 Personal Relationships: why information depends on personal relationships.

2.2.2 Mental Models: how mental models simplify decision-making.

2.2.3 Standard Terminology: how mental models must be shared to enable communication.

2.3 Personal Interactions: making progress through personal interactions.

2.3.1 Action and Reaction: how we advance based on how others react to our actions.

2.3.2 Reaction Unpredictability: why we can never exactly predict the reactions of others.

2.3.3 Likely Reactions: the range of potential reactions in gathering information.

2.3.4 Using Questions: using questions in gathering information and predicting reactions.

4.0 Leveraging Probability: making better decisions regarding our choice of opportunities.

4.3 Leveraging Form: how we can leverage the form of our territory.

4.3.1 Tilted Forms: opportunities that are dominated by uneven forces.

4.3.2 Fluid Forms: opportunities that are dominated by fast-changing directional forces.

4.3.3 Soft Forms: opportunities that are dominated by forces that create uncertainty.

4.3.4 Neutral Forms: opportunities where the terrain has no dominant forces.

4.4 Strategic Distance: relative proximity in strategic space.

4.4.1 Physical Distance: the issues of proximity in physical space.

4.4.2 Intellectual Distance: the challenges of moving through intellectual space.

Chapter 10

Field Position – Warning Signs

As you move into relationships, you discover their deeper nature. Each commitment is a stepping-stone to the next. Before you get more deeply involved in a relationship, you must judge whether or not it has a future. Sun Tzu uses six characteristics, called field positions, to evaluate your relationships for their future potential. These six characteristics tell you how easily you can maintain your relationship and advance it in the future.

In this adaptation we discuss these field positions as character types. The six types of character types—open, entangling, dependent, exclusive, protective, and uncommitted—are all extremes. They represent the extreme points in a three dimensional matrix of what Sun Tzu called "dangers, distance, and obstacles." For example, exclusive and uncommitted are the two extremes on the distance axis of this array. In real life, most situations are a combination of these factors, where conditions are somewhere between the two extremes.

The six flaws in relationships are amplified by the six extreme types of personality. You need to recognize and diagnose these weaknesses to predict how a given relationship will respond to a certain type of challenges in the future.

You must consider these issues in moving from one job position to another. As a career warrior, you must make good decisions as you move into new positions. Finally, you must compare your relative job situation with those of your opportunities before choosing any course of action.

The Art of War: Field Position

SUN TZU SAID:

Some field positions are unobstructed. 1
Some field positions are entangling.
Some field positions are supporting.
Some field positions are constricted.
Some field positions give you a barricade.
Some field positions are spread out.

7You can attack from some positions easily.
Other forces can meet you easily as well.
We call these unobstructed positions.
These positions are open.
On them, be the first to occupy a high, sunny area.
Put yourself where you can defend your supply routes.
Then you will have an advantage.

IN THE FIELD:

Strategy teaches that you can learn the true nature of a territory only once you have entered into it.

The Art of Love: **Warning Signs**

A LOVE SEEKER HEARS:

1 Some individuals are open.
Some individuals are entangling.
Some individuals are dependent.
Some individuals are exclusive.
Some individuals are protective.
Some individuals are uncommitted.

We can get close to some people easily.
Others can get close to these people as well.
These people have open personalities.
These people are open to relationships.
With one of these people, stay visible and optimistic.
Put yourself in situations where friends can support you.
Then you will have an opportunity for love.

TYPES:

There are six different types of people and each requires a different type of attention.

The Art of War: Field Position

¹⁴You can attack from some positions easily.
Disaster arises when you try to return to them.
These are entangling positions.
These field positions are one-sided.
Wait until your enemy is unprepared.
You can then attack from these positions and win.
Avoid a well-prepared enemy.
You will try to attack and lose.
Since you can't return, you will meet disaster.
These field positions offer no advantage.

²⁴You cannot leave some positions without losing an advantage.
If the enemy leaves this ground, he also loses an advantage.
We call these supporting field positions.
These positions strengthen you.
The enemy may try to entice you away.
Still, hold your position.
You must entice the enemy to leave.
You then strike him as he is leaving.
These field positions offer an advantage.

³³Some field positions are constricted.
Get to these positions first.
You must fill these areas and await the enemy.
Sometimes, the enemy will reach them first.
If he fills them, do not follow him.
However, if he fails to fill them, you can go after him.

The Art of Love: Warning Signs

We can get close to some people easily.
Disaster results when we lose our freedom.
Some people have entangling personalities.
Relationships with these people are one-sided.
Wait until a person like this grows bored.
You can then succeed in getting out of this relationship.
Avoid a needy relationship.
You can win a person's love and still lose.
If you are trapped, you will be unhappy.
This relationship offers no real opportunity for love.

We cannot breakup from some people without destroying our relationship with them.
If a rival breaks up with them, they will lose the relationship as well.
These are dependent personalities.
These relationships strengthen us.
We must avoid being enticed away from these people.
We must stay in these relationships.
We can be tempted by more exciting people.
We will then only have our heart broken.
These relationships offer a long-term opportunity.

Some individuals are exclusive.
These people become attached to their first love.
If their needs are satisfied, they are dependable.
Exclusive individuals focus on one relationship.
If they are satisfied, no one can win them away.
Only if they are neglected can they be tempted.

The Art of War: **Field Position**

³⁹Some field positions give you a barricade.
Get to these positions first.
You must occupy their southern, sunny heights in order to await the enemy.
Sometimes the enemy occupies these areas first.
If so, entice him away.
Never go after him.

⁴⁵Some field positions are too spread out.
Your force may seem equal to the enemy.
Still you will lose if you provoke a battle.
If you fight, you will not have any advantage.

⁴⁹These are the six types of field positions.
Each battleground has its own rules.
As a commander, you must know where to go.
You must examine each position closely.

2

Some armies can be outmaneuvered.
Some armies are too lax.
Some armies fall down.
Some armies fall apart.
Some armies are disorganized.
Some armies must retreat.

⁷Know all six of these weaknesses.
They create weak timing and disastrous positions.
They all arise from the army's commander.

YOUR FORCES:

The term "forces" means all elements used against the competition, both personnel and resources.

The Art of Love: **Warning Signs**

Some individuals are protective.
These people are ideal for a first love.
They desire a visible, happy relationship and are safe from temptation.
These people defend their relationships.
Their partners might be tempted away.
These individuals cannot be tempted.

Some individuals like being uncommitted.
People can try to develop relationships with them.
Nevertheless, they will never get a commitment from them.
These individuals are incapable of relationships.

These are the six types of personalities.
Each type of individual has its own rules.
To build a relationship, you must know who you are with.
You must evaluate each person carefully.

2 Some relationships can be blind-sided.
Some relationships are too loose.
Some relationships stumble.
Some relationships self-destruct.
Some relationships are chaotic.
Some relationships fade.

We must understand these six weaknesses.
Weak relationships can arise between good people.
Such weaknesses arise from personality defects.

> SYSTEMS:
>
> *Relationships are systems in which the parts must be put together to make sure that good stuff happens.*

The Art of War: **Field Position**

¹⁰One general can command a force equal to the enemy.
Still his enemy outflanks him.
This means that his army can be outmaneuvered.

¹³Another can have strong soldiers but weak officers.
This means that his army is too lax.

¹⁵Another has strong officers but weak soldiers.
This means that his army will fall down.

¹⁷Another has subcommanders that are angry and defiant.
They attack the enemy and fight their own battles.
The commander cannot know the battlefield.
This means that his army will fall apart.

²¹Another general is weak and easygoing.
He fails to make his orders clear.
His officers and men lack direction.
This shows in his military formations.
This means that his army is disorganized.

²⁶Another general fails to predict the enemy.
He pits his small forces against larger ones.
His weak forces attack stronger ones.
He fails to pick his fights correctly.
This means that his army must retreat.

Command:

Only one person makes the key decisions in an organization, thereby shaping it and creating any flaws.

The Art of Love: **Warning Signs**

Some relationships can look solid on the outside.
Still, outsiders can sneak into them.
This means that these relationships can be blind-sided.

Some people have good rapport but no shared goals.
These relationships are too loose.

Some people have shared goals but poor communication.
These relationships will stumble.

Sometimes individuals have their own priorities.
They want to get their own way in everything.
In these relationships, we never know where we stand.
These relationships will self-destruct.

Some individuals are lazy and sloppy.
They never know what they want.
Their goals and signals are unpredictable.
This shows in their relationships.
These relationships are chaotic.

Some individuals fail to understand their partners.
They put too much effort into unimportant issues.
They put too little effort into critical issues.
They make poor decisions.
These relationships will fade.

> **BALANCE:**
> *A relationship must balance work, communication, family, money, and romantic thinking.*

The Art of War: **Field Position**

³¹You must know all about these six weaknesses.
You must understand the philosophies that lead to defeat.
When a general arrives, you can know what he will do.
You must study each general carefully.

You must control your field position. **3**
It will always strengthen your army.

³You must predict the enemy to overpower him and win.
You must analyze the obstacles, dangers, and distances.
This is the best way to command.

⁶Understand your field position before you go to battle.
Then you will win.
You can fail to understand your field position and still fight.
Then you will lose.

¹⁰You must provoke battle when you will certainly win.
It doesn't matter what you are ordered.
The government may order you not to fight.
Despite that, you must always fight when you will win.

FORESIGHT:

Once you can quickly diagnose a situation, you know the appropriate response when others leave openings.

¹⁴Sometimes provoking a battle will lead to a loss.
The government may order you to fight.
Despite that, you must avoid battle when you will lose.

The Art of Love: **Warning Signs**

Be able to recognize these six weaknesses.
You must understand the thinking that leads to failure.
Within a relationship, you must know your partner.
You must evaluate their character carefully.

3 We must choose a compatible partner.
This is the foundation of a strong relationship.

We must truly know someone to commit to them.
We must appreciate their limits, problems, and needs.
This is the best way to win love.

Understand a person's deeper nature before commitment.
Then your love will last.
You can fail to see someone clearly and commit to them.
Then your love will fade.

We must commit only to people whose goals fit with ours.
Forget your infatuations.
You may not be attracted to the type of person you need.
Still, you must commit only to a compatible person.

Some personalities are simply all wrong for us.
We may be strongly attracted to this type of person.
Still, we must avoid these people if we want true love.

We must never seek commitment to satisfy our egos.

FLEXIBILITY:

As we learn more about our situation, we must be willing to adapt our plans accordingly.

The Art of War: **Field Position**

¹⁷You must advance without desiring praise.
You must retreat without fearing shame.
The only correct move is to preserve your troops.
This is how you serve your country.
This is how you reward your nation.

Think of your soldiers as little children. 4
You can make them follow you into a deep river.
Treat them as your beloved children.
You can lead them all to their deaths.

⁵Some leaders are generous but cannot use their men.
They love their men but cannot command them.
Their men are unruly and disorganized.
These leaders create spoiled children.
Their soldiers are useless.

You may know what your soldiers will do in an attack. 5
You may not know if the enemy is vulnerable to attack.
You will then win only half the time.
You may know that the enemy is vulnerable to attack.
You may not know if your men have the capability of attacking him.
You will still win only half the time.
You may know that the enemy is vulnerable to attack.
You may know that your men are ready to attack.
You may not, however, know how to position yourself in the field for battle.
You will still win only half the time.

The Art of Love: **Warning Signs**

We must leave bad relationships without embarrassment.
The only correct move is to protect our future.
This is how we find happiness.
This is how we ensure love.

4 We must be able to trust love like little children.
It must be solid even when everything else is changing.
Treat your relationship like a rare prize.
You hold life in your hands.

Some people are too giving and are taken for granted.
They care for others but don't demand anything in return.
Their partners take advantage of them.
These people spoil their relationships.
Their devotion is wasted.

5 We may know what we can offer in a relationship.
Nevertheless, we may not know what our lover needs.
Then our relationship will work only half the time.
We can know what our lover needs.
Nevertheless, we may not know if we have the ability to satisfy those needs.
Then our relationship will work only half the time.
We can know what our lover needs.
We can know that we are ready to give it.
Nevertheless, we may not know if how to move to a position where our connection can be made.
Still our relationships will work only half the time

The Art of War: **Field Position**

¹¹You must know how to make war.
You can then act without confusion.
You can attempt anything.

¹⁴We say:
Know the enemy and know yourself.
Your victory will be painless.
Know the weather and the field.
Your victory will be complete.

RELATIVITY:

Strategically, all your qualities, both good and bad, arise only in comparison with your opponents.

The Art of Love: **Warning Signs**

You must know how to win lasting love.
You can then trust with certainty.
You can have complete confidence.

We say this:
Know your lover and yourself.
Your relationship will be painless.
Know your temperaments and personalities.
Your relationship will be complete.

◆ ◆ ◆

SYNTHESIS:

Seeking love acknowledges that we cannot know everything but that we must master a few key elements.

Related Articles from *Sun Tzu's Playbook*

In chapter ten, Sun Tzu discusses the use of temporary positions in building relationships with voters. To learn the step-by-step techniques involved, we recommend the Sun Tzu's Art of War Playbook *articles listed below.*

2.3 Personal Interactions: making progress through personal interactions.

2.3.1 Action and Reaction: how we advance based on how others reaction to our actions.

2.3.2 Reaction Unpredictability: why we can never exactly predict the react of others.

2.3.3 Likely Reactions: the range of potential reactions in gathering information.

2.3.4 Using Questions: using questions in gathering information and predicting reactions.

4.5 Opportunity Surfaces: judging potential opportunities from a distance.

4.5.1 Surface Area: choosing opportunities on the basis of their size.

4.5.2 Surface Barriers: how to select opportunities by evaluating obstacles.

4.5.3 Surface Holding Power: sticky and slippery situations.

4.6 Six Benchmarks: simplifying the comparisons of opportunities.

4.6.1 Spread-Out Conditions: recognizing opportunities that are too large.

4.6.2 Constricted Conditions: identifying and using constricted positions.

4.6.3 Barricaded Conditions: the issues related to the extremes of obstacles.

4.6.4 Wide-Open Conditions: the issues related to an absence of barriers.

4.6.5 Fixed Conditions: positions with extreme holding power.

4.6.6 Sensitive Conditions: positions with no holding power on pursuing opportunities.

4.7 Competitive Weakness: how certain opportunities can bring out our weaknesses.

4.7.1 Command Weaknesses: the character flaws of leaders and how to exploit them.

4.7.2 Group Weaknesses: organizational weakness and where groups fail.

4.8 Climate Support: choosing new positions based on future changes.

4.9 Opportunity Mapping: two-dimensional tool for comparing opportunity probabilities.

Chapter 11

Types of Terrain – Relationship Stages

As a relationship moves forward, it passes through nine common situations or stages. Each of these stages poses a specific type of challenge. Each of these challenges requires a specific response. The key to moving forward successfully is instantly recognizing and reacting to these situations as they arise. Inappropriate reactions make each of these situations worse and slow down your progress. Since speed is the essence of war, you must train yourself to instantly recognize these situations and to respond by reflex.

In these stages, the earliest steps are usually the easiest and you have the most options. As you make progress, the challenges get more difficult. You have fewer and fewer options until the final stages, which are the most difficult and desperate.

The increasing difficulty of a relationship over time makes sense because each step forward takes you deeper into commitment. The pressure on the relationship grows. At the beginning, your involvement are relatively casual and you have little control over your future. As you move further and further along a romantic path, more and more complications arise.

Through the entire process, you must maintain the pace of progress. A good decision maker learns how to use the increasing pressures of the relationship to unify and focus it. The psychological pressures of getting closer can destroy a relationship if you don't immediately know how to respond.

The Art of War: Types of Terrain

GROUND:

Ground, territory, and terrain are all from the same Chinese concept, "di," which also means situation and condition.

SUN TZU SAID:

Use the art of war. 1
Know when the terrain will scatter you.
Know when the terrain will be easy.
Know when the terrain will be disputed.
Know when the terrain is open.
Know when the terrain is intersecting.
Know when the terrain is dangerous.
Know when the terrain is bad.
Know when the terrain is confined.
Know when the terrain is deadly.

11Warring parties must sometimes fight inside their own territory.
This is scattering terrain.

13When you enter hostile territory, your penetration is shallow.
This is easy terrain.

15Some terrain gives you an advantageous position.
But it gives others an advantageous position as well.
This will be disputed terrain.

The Art of Love: Relationship Stages

A LOVE SEEKER HEARS:

1 Use the skills of love.
Know when your relationship is tenuous.
Know when your relationship is easy.
Know when your relationship is competitive.
Know when your relationship is open.
Know when your relationship is shared.
Know when your relationship is serious.
Know when your relationship is difficult.
Know when your relationship is committed.
Know when your relationship is do-or-die.

People new to a relationship sometimes fight for their own space.
This is a tenuous relationship.

When we are new to a relationship, commitment is limited.
This is an easy relationship.

We can have a good relationship with someone.
Nevertheless, a rival can have a close relationship as well.
This is a competitive relationship.

STAGES:

The nine stages described here explain a logical evolution that relationships go through as they continue.

The Art of War: Types of Terrain

¹⁸You can use some terrain to advance easily.
Others can advance along with you.
This is open terrain.

²¹Everyone shares access to a given area.
The first one to arrive there can gather a larger group than anyone else.
This is intersecting terrain.

²⁴You can penetrate deeply into hostile territory.
Then many hostile cities are behind you.
This is dangerous terrain.

²⁷There are mountain forests.
There are dangerous obstructions.
There are reservoirs.
Everyone confronts these obstacles on a campaign.
They make bad terrain.

³²In some areas, the entry passage is narrow.
You are closed in as you try to get out of them.
In this type of area, a few people can effectively attack your much larger force.
This is confined terrain.

³⁶You can sometimes survive only if you fight quickly.
You will die if you delay.
This is deadly terrain.

The Art of Love: Relationship Stages

We feel we are making progress in a relationship.
New rivals, however, can still come in at any time.
This is an open relationship.

Friends and family are interested in meeting us.
If we develop good relations with these people, it will bring us closer.
This is the shared stage of a relationship.

We have gotten deeply involved with someone.
They still don't know if they can trust us.
This is the serious stage of a relationship.

Our shared future is in doubt.
We have squabbles.
Feelings are uncertain.
Everyone encounters such difficulties in building a relationship.
This is the difficult stage in a relationship.

In a relationship, there are key transition points.
A commitment must be made to get through them.
Everything invested in a relationship can be lost if an attractive rival appears.
This is the commitment stage of a relationship.

Sometimes the relationship cannot continue without a sacrifice.
The relationship will die if we wait.
This is the do-or-die stage of a relationship.

The Art of War: **Types of Terrain**

³⁹To be successful, you must control scattering terrain by avoiding battle.
Control easy terrain by not stopping.
Control disputed terrain by not attacking.
Control open terrain by staying with the enemy's forces.
Control intersecting terrain by uniting with your allies.
Control dangerous terrain by plundering.
Control bad terrain by keeping on the move.
Control confined terrain by using surprise.
Control deadly terrain by fighting.

Go to an area that is known to be good for waging war. **2**
Use it to cut off the enemy's contact between his front and back lines.
Prevent his small parties from relying on his larger force.
Stop his strong divisions from rescuing his weak ones.
Prevent his officers from getting their men together.
Chase his soldiers apart to stop them from amassing.
Harass them to prevent their ranks from forming.

⁸When joining battle gives you an advantage, you must do it.
When it isn't to your benefit, you must avoid it.

CONTROL:

Each of the nine "terrains," "conditions," or "stages" demands a specific form of response.

¹⁰A daring soldier may ask:
"A large, organized enemy army and its general are coming.
What do I do to prepare for them?"

The Art of Love: Relationship Stages

To win love, avoid tenuous relationships by not getting involved in them.
In the easy relationship, don't stop making progress.
In the competitive relationship, do not criticize others.
In the open relationship, keep up with your rivals.
In the shared stage, bond with family and friends.
In the serious stage, become more intimate.
In the difficult stage, form emotional ties.
In the commitment stage, use surprise.
In the do-or-die stage, fight for the relationship.

2 Get involved with a person with whom you are compatible
You must be able to both win this person's affection and satisfy their needs.
You can win someone over a step at a time.
Satisfy needs when another is feeling neglected.
Prevent fears and insecurities from being realized.
Keep a partner too busy to spend time with others.
You can move quickly to overcome resistance.

If spending time together is comfortable, you must do it.
If time together isn't comfortable, you avoid it.

You may tell yourself,
"I have rivals that are much more established and appealing I am.
 What can I do?"

> **DREAMS:**
>
> *Dreams never come true because successful dreams simply lead to even better dreams of the future.*

The Art of War: Types of Terrain

¹³Tell him:
"First seize an area that the enemy must have.
Then he will pay attention to you.
Mastering speed is the essence of war.
Take advantage of a large enemy's inability to keep up.
Use a philosophy of avoiding difficult situations.
Attack the area where he doesn't expect you."

3 You must use the philosophy of an invader.
Invade deeply and then concentrate your forces.
This controls your men without oppressing them.

⁴Get your supplies from the riches of the territory.
It is sufficient to supply your whole army.

⁶Take care of your men and do not overtax them.
Your esprit de corps increases your momentum.
Keep your army moving and plan for surprises.
Make it difficult for the enemy to count your forces.
Position your men where there is no place to run.
They will then face death without fleeing.
They will find a way to survive.
Your officers and men will fight to their utmost.

¹⁴Military officers who are committed lose their fear.
When they have nowhere to run, they must stand firm.
Deep in enemy territory, they are captives.
Since they cannot escape, they will fight.

The Art of Love: **Relationship Stages**

Tell yourself this"
You can quickly win a special place in your intended's heart.
Then rivals can try to undermine you.
Moving quickly is the essence of romance.
Take advantage of an appealing rival's inability to commit.
Make it your goal to build comfortable relationship.
Change the relationship while rivals are unprepared.

3 We must have the goal of becoming part of someone's life.
Get deeply involved with your beloved and focus on them.
This influences them without coercing them.

We can get everything we need from a single relationship.
The right person can fulfill us in every way.

Sharpen your sensitivities and don't stretch yourself too thin.
Creating a partnership deepens your emotional bonds.
Keep your relationship moving forward and plan for surprises.
Make it difficult for your lover to take you for granted.
You must be willing to commit to the permanence of marriage.
You must then face problems in the marriage without leaving.
You will then find a way to overcome them.
In marriage, your commitment makes the critical difference.

When you marry, you lose your fear of intimacy.
Deeply committed, you can stand up for yourself.
In a committed marriage, people are more devoted.
When the relationship is lifelong, you must fight for it.

The Art of War: Types of Terrain

¹⁸Commit your men completely.
Without being posted, they will be on guard.
Without being asked, they will get what is needed.
Without being forced, they will be dedicated.
Without being given orders, they can be trusted.

²³Stop them from guessing by removing all their doubts.
Stop them from dying by giving them no place to run.

²⁵Your officers may not be rich.
Nevertheless, they still desire plunder.
They may die young.
Nevertheless, they still want to live forever.

²⁹You must order the time of attack.
Officers and men may sit and weep until their lapels are wet.
When they stand up, tears may stream down their cheeks.
Put them in a position where they cannot run.
They will show the greatest courage under fire.

Make good use of war. 4
This demands instant reflexes.
You must develop these instant reflexes.
Act like an ordinary mountain snake.
If people strike your head then stop them with your tail.
If they strike your tail then stop them with your head.
If they strike your middle then use both your head and tail.

The Art of Love: **Relationship Stages**

Commit yourself completely to your marriage.
Without being told, you must see what needs to be done.
Without being asked, you will know what to say.
Without being pressured, you must be affectionate.
Without being watched, you must be trustworthy.

Stop any second-guessing by never considering divorce.
Avoid failure by leaving yourself no excuses.

You may not be rich or beautiful.
Nevertheless, you deserve lasting love.
Your marriage can fail.
It shouldn't be because you were not committed to it.

You must know when it is time to advance the relationship.
You may be afraid to commit yourself for a relationship.
You may be terrified of a breakup.
Commit so that you cannot run from problems.
You can be devoted to your lover.

4 Make good use of preparation.
This demands instant reflexes.
You must know how to react beforehand.
You must be quick and flexible.
Someone may challenge your thinking. defend with your feelings.
Someone may challenge your feelings, defend with your thinking.
If they challenge your character, defend your head and your heart.

The Art of War: **Types of Terrain**

⁸A daring soldier asks:
"Can any army imitate these instant reflexes?"
We answer:
"It can."

¹²To command and get the most out of proud people, you must study adversity.
People work together when they are in the same boat during a storm.
In this situation, one rescues the other just as the right hand helps the left.

ADVERSITY:

Strategically, unity is strength, and nothing unites a force more than being threatened by a common enemy.

¹⁵Use adversity correctly.
Tether your horses and bury your wagon's wheels.
Still, you can't depend on this alone.
An organized force is braver than lone individuals.
This is the art of organization.
Put the tough and weak together.
You must also use the terrain.

²²Make good use of war.
Unite your men as one.
Never let them give up.

The commander must be a military professional. **5**
This requires confidence and detachment.
You must maintain dignity and order.
You must control what your men see and hear.
They must follow you without knowing your plans.

The Art of Love: Relationship Stages

You may ask yourself,
Do I always have to instantly defend my mate?
There is only one answer.
You must!

For two people to join together as a true team, you must both share adversity.
Remember that both you and your spouse truly need one another.
You should help one another as naturally as your right hand helps your left.

Respond well under pressure.
Show your willingness to sacrifice for the marriage.
Even this isn't enough.
Try to become a true partner with your mate.
This is the art of marriage.
Use each other's strengths to minimize weaknesses.
You must depend on your relationship.

> **LEADERSHIP:**
>
> *We position ourselves for leadership when our decision-making focuses on our lover's concerns.*

Make good use of your marriage.
Come together as one.
Never let each other give up.

5 We must be realistic about romance.
This requires confidence and pragmatism.
We must maintain our dignity and values.
We must control what our spouse sees and hears.
Our spouse must trust us without knowing every thought.

The Art of War: **Types of Terrain**

⁶You can reinvent your men's roles.
You can change your plans.
You can use your men without their understanding.

⁹You must shift your campgrounds.
You must take detours from the ordinary routes.
You must use your men without giving them your strategy.

¹²A commander provides what is needed now.
This is like climbing high and being willing to kick away your ladder.
You must be able to lead your men deeply into different surrounding territory.
And yet, you can discover the opportunity to win.

¹⁶You must drive men like a flock of sheep.
You must drive them to march.
You must drive them to attack.
You must never let them know where you are headed.
You must unite them into a great army.
You must then drive them against all opposition.
This is the job of a true commander.

²³You must adapt to the different terrain.
You must adapt to find an advantage.
You must manage your people's affections.
You must study all these skills.

The Art of Love: **Relationship Stages**

As a couple, we can reinvent our roles.
We can change our plans.
We can reshape our relationship without planning.

As a couple, we must make a new home.
We can find a way to change our old habits.
We can be willing to accept decisions on trust alone.

We must provide what our mate needs at the moment.
We must be willing to go out on a limb and take a risk for the relationship.
We must get deeply involved with our spouse's feeling to identify the needs that create the opportunity that we need to get closer.

We must work to make any marriage successful.

We must work at staying together.
We must work toward mutual goals.
Neither of us must worry about where we are headed.
We must unite as a single, powerful team.
Together, we must work to overcome problems.
This is the hallmark of a successful marriage.

We must adapt to every stage in our relationship.
We must adjust to keep the relationship working.
We must know how to keep someone's affections.
We must master all these skills.

The Art of War: Types of Terrain

Always use the philosophy of invasion. 6
Deep invasions concentrate your forces.
Shallow invasions scatter your forces.
When you leave your country and cross the border, you must take control.
This is always critical ground.
You can sometimes move in any direction.
This is always intersecting ground.
You can penetrate deeply into a territory.
This is always dangerous ground.
You penetrate only a little way.
This is always easy ground.
Your retreat is closed and the path ahead tight.
This is always confined ground.
There is sometimes no place to run.
This is always deadly ground.

[16]To use scattering terrain correctly, you must inspire your men's devotion.
On easy terrain, you must keep in close communication.
On disputed terrain, you must hamper the enemy's progress.
On open terrain, you must carefully defend your chosen position.
On intersecting terrain, you must solidify your alliances.
On dangerous terrain, you must ensure your food supplies.
On bad terrain, you must keep advancing along the road.
On confined terrain, you must stop information leaks from your headquarters.
On deadly terrain, you must show what you can do by killing the enemy.

The Art of Love: **Relationship Stages**

6 We must always be deeply committed to our marriage.
Commitment to the relationship focuses our efforts.
Weak commitments dissipate our efforts.
At the beginning of a relationship, we must use self-control to avoid conflict.
This is a critical stage.
Our relationship then can go in any direction.
This is the shared stage of relationship.
We get deeply involved with one another.
This is the serious stage.
People always seem interesting when we first meet them.
This is the easy stage of a relationship.
We eventually get close and foresee a life together.
This the committed stage of a relationship.
Once married, we are bonded forever.
This is the do-or-die stage.

To succeed in the tenuous stage, we must show our devotion to our lover.
In the easy stage, we must communicate frequently.
At the competitive stage, create obstacles for any possible rivals.
In the open stage, build bonds and prove our devotion.
In the shared stage, we must bond with friends and relatives.
In the serious stage, we must meet each other's needs.
In the difficult stage, we must keep moving forward.
In the committed stage, we must build a foundation for a lasting relationship.
In the do-or-die stage, we must prove ourselves by continually deserving love.

The Art of War: **Types of Terrain**

²⁵Make your men feel like an army.
Surround them and they will defend themselves.
If they cannot avoid it, they will fight.
If they are under pressure, they will obey.

7

Do the right thing when you don't know your different enemies' plans.
Don't attempt to meet them.

³You don't know the position of mountain forests, dangerous obstructions, and reservoirs?
Then you cannot march the army.
You don't have local guides?
You won't get any of the benefits of the terrain.

⁷There are many factors in war.
You may lack knowledge of any one of them.
If so, it is wrong to take a nation into war.

¹⁰You must be able to control your government's war.
If you divide a big nation, it will be unable to put together a large force.
Increase your enemy's fear of your ability.
Prevent his forces from getting together and organizing.

KNOWLEDGE:

Strategy teaches that you can replace investment of time and effort with more complete information.

The Art of Love: **Relationship Stages**

We make our partner feel like part of a team.
If we are tied together, we will defend one another.
When we cannot divorce, we will make the relationship work.
When we share difficulties, we bond.

7 Do the right thing when you don't understand a potential lover's thinking:
Don't try to win affection from them.

We don't understand the other person's priorities, problems, and shortcomings?
Then we should not get involved with them.
We don't have mutual friends?
We won't get any help in our relationship.

There is so much to know in building a relationship.
We must look honestly at every situation.
If we cannot, it is foolish to think that we are in love.

We must be able to influence the object of our affections.
Split the difference in any big issues before they become a problem in the relationship.
Increase your lover's concern.
Prevent problems from compounding and growing over time.

> **REEVALUATE:**
>
> *Relationship analysis must be repeated as we reexamine the five key factors that define our position.*

The Art of War: **Types of Terrain**

¹⁴Do the right thing and do not arrange outside alliances before their time.
You will not have to assert your authority prematurely.
Trust only yourself and your self-interest.
This increases the enemy's fear of you.
You can make one of his allies withdraw.
His whole nation can fall.

²⁰Distribute rewards without worrying about having a system.
Halt without the government's command.
Attack with the whole strength of your army.
Use your army as if it were a single man.

²⁴Attack with skill.
Do not discuss it.
Attack when you have an advantage.
Do not talk about the dangers.
When you can launch your army into deadly ground, even if it stumbles, it can still survive.
You can be weakened in a deadly battle and yet be stronger afterward.

³⁰Even a large force can fall into misfortune.
If you fall behind, however, you can still turn defeat into victory.
You must use the skills of war.
To survive, you must adapt yourself to your enemy's purpose.
You must stay with him no matter where he goes.
It may take a thousand miles to kill the general.
If you correctly understand him, you can find the skill to do it.

The Art of Love: **Relationship Stages**

Act correctly and don't rely heavily on the involvement of friends and family.
Then you won't have to battle over who is right.
Trust each other and yourselves as a team.
Don't tell your families everything about your relationship.
Don't force a partner to take sides against family members.
Your whole relationship could collapse.

Be generous with each other without splitting everything equally.
Stop fighting about who makes the decisions.
Dedicate your whole strength to making the relationship work.
Think of yourself and your mate as a single person.

Be skilled in moving into new areas.
Do not discuss it.
Invite intimacy when you have something to share.
Don't worry about the problems.
Relationships are difficult, but even if we have problems we can keep our relationship alive.
We can get hurt by getting close, but we are stronger for it afterward.

Even a good relationship can get into trouble.
If we get into trouble, use problems to create emotional bonds.
We must use our skills at romance.
To succeed, we must adapt to our lover's needs.
We must be able to stay together wherever life leads.
We can share thousands of setbacks.
If we understand each other, we can make the relationship work.

The Art of War: Types of Terrain

Manage your government correctly at the start of a war. **8**
Close your borders and tear up passports.
Block the passage of envoys.
Encourage politicians at headquarters to stay out of it.
You must use any means to put an end to politics.
Your enemy's people will leave you an opening.
You must instantly invade through it.

⁸Immediately seize a place that they love.
Do it quickly.
Trample any border to pursue the enemy.
Use your judgment about when to fight.

¹²Doing the right thing at the start of war is like approaching a woman.
Your enemy's men must open the door.
After that, you should act like a streaking rabbit.
The enemy will be unable to catch you.

BEGINNINGS:

The start of a campaign is a delicate time when you set the direction for the entire course of the campaign.

The Art of Love: **Relationship Stages**

8 Do the right things at the start of a relationship.
Narrow your focus and forget other people.
Don't communicate indirectly.
Have families and friends stay out of it.
Use any means available to avoid squabbling.
Eventually you will find an opportunity to get closer.
You must instantly take advantage of it.

Quickly win your sweetheart's affection.
Waste no time.
Ignore barriers to pursue the relationship.
Use your best judgment about when to commit.

Success at the start of a new relationship requires becoming a focus of attention.
Your sweetheart must eventually give you an opening.
When you have the opportunity, you should act quickly.
Your insecurities will be unable to catch up with you.

OPENINGS:

> *We cannot win love without the cooperation of others who create the openings that we need to move forward.*

Related Articles from *Sun Tzu's Playbook*

In chapter eleven, Sun Tzu explains instant situation response. To learn the step-by-step techniques involved, we recommend the Sun Tzu's Art of War Playbook *articles listed below.*

6.0 Situation Response: selecting the actions most appropriate to a situation.

6.1 Situation Recognition: situation recognition in making advances.

6.1.1 Conditioned Reflexes: how we develop automatic, instantaneous responses.

6.1.2 Prioritizing Conditions: parsing complex competitive conditions into simple responses.

6.2 Campaign Evaluation: how we justify continued investment in an ongoing campaign.

6.2.1 Campaign Flow: seeing campaigns as a series of situations that flow logically from one to another.

6.2.2 Campaign Goals: assessing the value of a campaign by a larger mission.

6.3 Campaign Patterns: how knowing campaign stages gives us insight into our situation.

6.3.1 Early-Stage Situations: the common situations that arise the earliest in campaigns.

6.3.2 Middle-Stage Situations: how progress creates transitional situations in campaigns.

6.3.3 Late-Stage Situations: understanding the final and most dangerous stages of campaigns.

6.4 Nine Situations: the nine common competitive situations.

6.4.1 Dissipating Situations: situations where defensive unity is destroyed.

6.4.2 Easy Situations: recognizing situations of easy initial progress.

6.4.3 Contentious Situations: identifying situations that invite conflict.

6.4.4 Open Situations: recognizing situations that are races without a course.

6.4.5 Intersecting Situations: recognizing situations that bring people together.

6.4.6 Serious Situations: identifying situations where resources can be cut off.

6.4.7 Difficult Situations: recognizing situations where serious barriers must be overcome.

6.4.8 Limited Situations: identifying situations defined by a bottleneck.

6.4.9 Desperate Situations: identifying situations where destruction is possible.

6.5 Nine Responses: using the best responses to the nine common competitive situations.

6.5.1 Dissipating Response: responding to dissipation by the use of offense as defense.

6.5.2 Easy Response: responding to easy situations by overcoming complacency.

6.5.3 Contentious Response: responding to contentious situations by knowing how to avoid conflict.

6.5.4 Open Response: responding to open situations by keeping up with the opposition.

6.5.5 Intersecting Response: the formation of situational alliances.

6.5.6 Serious Response: responding to serious situations by finding immediate income.

6.5.7 Difficult Response: the role of persistence in responding to difficult situations.

6.5.8 Limited Response: the need for secret speed in limited situations.

6.5.9 Desperate Response: using all our resources in responding to desperate situations.

6.6 Campaign Pause: knowing when to stop advancing a position.

Chapter 12

火攻

Attacking With Fire – Heart's Desire

Although Sun Tzu uses this chapter to cover a specific weapon, fire, its broader subject is using any weapon, with an emphasis on leveraging forces in the environment as weapons. For building relationships, this chapter serves as a guide to use the most important interpersonal weapon of all: people's desires.

In Sun Tzu's system, creation and destruction are united. We cannot create without destroying. We create satisfaction with a relationship by destroying desires. You start this process by picking a target. There are five potential types of targets for fire or desire. Desire takes many forms, from physical passion to the desire for companionship.

Changes in the emotional climate make these use of these weapons possible. Timing is critical in finding an opportunity for using desire. You cannot target one set of desires until people have satisfied other sets ones. The targeting of desire itself is less important than the response to it. You cannot create the opportunity for targeting a desire. It is only found in someone else. It is the response to desire that creates the opportunity.

Creative change, symbolized by water, is also an environmental weapon, but the use of destructive change, symbolized by fire, has advantages that creative change cannot match. All change is emotional. Change creates the fear of the unknown. Passion is especially frightening. You need to control your emotional responses in both undertaking and responding to these attacks.

The Art of War: Attacking With Fire

FIRE:

Classical strategy describes the element of fire as a weapon and uses it as a metaphor for all weapons.

SUN TZU SAID:

There are five ways of attacking with fire. 1
The first is burning troops.
The second is burning supplies.
The third is burning supply transport.
The fourth is burning storehouses.
The fifth is burning camps.

7To make fire, you must have the resources.
To build a fire, you must prepare the raw materials.

9To attack with fire, you must be in the right season.
To start a fire, you must have the time.

11Choose the right season.
The weather must be dry.

13Choose the right time.
Pick a season when the grass is as high as the side of a cart.

15You can tell the proper days by the stars in the night sky.
You want days when the wind rises in the morning.

The Art of Love: **Heart's Desire**

A Love Seeker hears:

1 There are five ways to kindle desire.
The first is inciting physical passion.
The second is offering security.
The third is offering recognition.
The fourth is offering wealth.
The fifth is offering companionship.

To create desire, we must have the right attributes.
To build desire, we must create the right mood and frame of mind.

To arouse excitement, we must pick the right time.
To incite passion, we must invest our time.

Choose the right time.
Your intended must feel the need.

Be careful of your timing.
Your beloved must have time to relax.

To know the right time, try to uncover hidden desires.
Pick the time when a beloved's desire is building.

.

Desires:

The targets for using desire as a weapon are the same as the different types of resources people value.

The Art of War: Attacking With Fire

Everyone attacks with fire. 2
You must create five different situations with fire and be able to adjust to them.

³You start a fire inside the enemy's camp.
Then attack the enemy's periphery.

⁵You launch a fire attack, but the enemy remains calm.
Wait and do not attack.

⁷The fire reaches its height.
Follow its path if you can.
If you can't follow it, stay where you are.

REACTION:

The environment is unpredictable so you must always act based upon how situations develop rather than your plans.

¹⁰Spreading fires on the outside of camp can kill.
You can't always get fire inside the enemy's camp.
Take your time in spreading it.

¹³Set the fire when the wind is at your back.
Don't attack into the wind.
Daytime winds last a long time.
Night winds fade quickly.

¹⁷Every army must know how to adjust to the five possible attacks by fire.
Use many men to guard against them.

The Art of Love: **Heart's Desire**

2 Everyone tries to use sex appeal.
We must be able to use five different approaches and respond to these approaches.

We make someone aware of what we offer.
Then we make light physical contact.

We try to stimulate desire, but there is no response.
We must wait and bide our time.

Desire builds over time.
We can utilize the opening that desire creates for us.
If passion doesn't create an opening, be patient.

We can flirt with at a distance to create excitement.
We can't always make direct contact.
Take your time arousing interest.

Use sex appeal when the atmosphere supports it.
Don't work against the mood of the moment.
Public romantic moments are long lasting.
Private romantic moods fade quickly.

You must master these five approaches to arousing a person's desires.
You must be constantly prepared to use these methods.

> CONTROL:
> *The less control we have over the way that others react, the more control we must have over the way that we react.*

The Art of War: **Attacking With Fire**

When you use fire to assist your attacks, you are clever. 3
Water can add force to an attack.
You can also use water to disrupt an enemy.
It does not, however, take his resources.

You win in battle by getting the opportunity to attack. 4
It is dangerous if you fail to study how to accomplish this achievement.
As commander, you cannot waste your opportunities.

[4]We say:
A wise leader plans success.
A good general studies it.
If there is little to be gained, don't act.
If there is little to win, do not use your men.
If there is no danger, don't fight.

[10]As leader, you cannot let your anger interfere with the success of your forces.
As commander, you cannot let yourself become enraged before you go to battle.
Join the battle only when it is in your advantage to act.
If there is no advantage in joining a battle, stay put.

DECISION:

Your decisions must use the emotion of others. Your emotions cannot determine your decisions.

The Art of Love: **Heart's Desire**

3 When we use desire to assist our advances, we are being smart.
Personality can help our cause.
We can also use our personality to get attention.
Personality alone doesn't, however, inspire passion.

4 We keep love by finding opportunities to share intimacy.
It is a mistake not to devote time required to making yourself attractive.
In keeping love, you cannot grow careless.

We say this:
A smart lover foresees love.
A good partner studies it.
If there is no time for love, don't make a pass.
If love isn't fun, don't waste your efforts.
If there is no danger, don't fight against love.

We must never let our mood interfere with the building of emotional bonds.
As a lover, we cannot fight simply because our feelings are hurt.
Join in conflict only when something important is at stake.
If there is no chance to improve the relationship, keep quiet.

> **SUCCESS:**
> *A great relationship is not one that win others' recognition. It is one that makes us both happy.*

The Art of War: **Attacking With Fire**

¹⁴Anger can change back into happiness.
Rage can change back into joy.
A nation once destroyed cannot be brought back to life.
Dead men do not return to the living.

¹⁸This fact must make a wise leader cautious.
A good general is on guard.

²⁰Your philosophy must be to keep the nation peaceful and the army intact.

EMOTION:

Emotional gratification is never the goal of a competition. You must never lose sight of your goals in the heat of battle.

The Art of Love: **Heart's Desire**

All emotions shift over time.
Even hatred can change into affection.
A relationship once destroyed cannot come back to life.
A broken heart never truly heals.

Knowing this, we must be careful.
A serious lover is always on guard.

Our goal must be to keep our relationships productive and to look better than any altern

THE PAYOFF:

Desire, like all weapons, cuts both ways. Another's desires can be rewarding. Our own desires can be costly.

Related Articles from *Sun Tzu's Playbook*

In chapter twelve, Sun Tzu discusses the use of environmental weapons. To learn the step-by-step techniques involved, we recommend the Sun Tzu's Art of War Playbook articles listed below.

9.0 Understanding Vulnerability: the use of common environmental attacks.

9.1 Climate Vulnerability: our vulnerability to environmental crises arising from change.

9.1.1 Climate Rivals: how changing conditions create opponents.

9.1.2 Threat Development: how changing conditions create environmental threats.

9.2 Points of Vulnerability: our points of vulnerability during an environmental crisis.

9.2.1 Personnel Risk: the vulnerability of key individuals.

9.2.2 Immediate Resource Risk: the vulnerability of the resources required for immediate use.

9.2.3 Transportation/Communication Risk: how firestorms choke normal channels of movement and communication.

9.2.4 Asset Risk: the threats to our fixed assets.

9.2.5 Organizational Risk: targeting the roles and responsibilities within an organization.

9.3 Crisis Leadership: maintaining the support of our supporters during attacks.

9.3.1 Mutual Danger: how we use mutual danger to create mutual strength.

9.3.2 Message Control: communication methods to use during a crisis.

9.4 Crisis Defense: how vulnerabilities are exploited and defended during a crisis.

9.4.1 Division Defense: preventing organizational division during a crisis.

9.4.2 Panic Defense: preventing the mistakes arising from panic during a crisis.

9.4.3 Defending Openings: how to defend openings created by a crisis.

9.4.4 Defending Alliances: dealing with guilt by association.

9.4.5 Defensive Balance: using short-term conditions to tip the balance in a crisis.

9.5 Crisis Exploitation: how to successfully use an opponent's crisis.

9.5.1 Adversarial Opportunities: how our opponents' crises can create opportunities.

9.5.2 Avoiding Emotion: the danger of exploiting environmental vulnerabilities for purely emotion reasons.

9.6 Constant Vigilance: where to focus our attention to preserve our positions.

Chapter 13

Using Spies — Knowing Another

Sun Tzu sees communication as critical to success. In romantic comparisons, communication is essential both to meeting people and to getting to know someone. This final chapter emphasizes this by returning us to the starting point for relationship analysis: gathering information. Though we traditionally translate this idea in terms of spies, the original Chinese term actually means "go-between" or "conduit" of information.

The many risks in relationships can be minimized by the right information. The entire science of strategy is built around the idea that you use information to replace the more costly assets of time, effort, and other resources. Information guides you toward the doing the right things as well as teaching you how to do things right.

This information must come from people because issues of character are largely subjective, not easily boiled down to objective criteria. Often, you can get it only from your romantic partner. Only people can tell you what they are thinking.

There are five different types of information, based on the five key factors introduced in the first chapter. Gathering this information is not a passive process. It requires people management skills. Before you tackle a specific relationship problem, you must get a complete picture of that problem. Your partner may have that information, but people often have a very poor perspective on their own situation. The most successful people are those who are the most skillful at communication and cultivating good information sources.

The Art of War: Using Spies

SUN TZU SAID:

All successful armies require thousands of men. 1
They invade and march thousands of miles.
Whole families are destroyed.
Other families must be heavily taxed.
Every day, a large amount of money must be spent.

⁶Internal and external events force people to move.
They are unable to work while on the road.
They are unable to find and hold a useful job.
This affects 70 percent of thousands of families.

¹⁰You can watch and guard for years.
Then a single battle can determine victory in a day.
Despite this, bureaucrats worship the value of
their salary money too dearly.
They remain ignorant of the enemy's condition.
The result is cruel.

¹⁵They are not leaders of men.
They are not servants of the state.
They are not masters of victory.

ECONOMICS:

The science of strategy is based on the idea that better information can be used to eliminate other costs.

The Art of Love: **Knowing Another**

A LOVE SEEKER HEARS:

1 Developing a relationship requires thousands of hours.
We have to work through thousands of problems.
Most relationships are doomed.
Many relationships are seriously strained.
Every year, thousands of dollars are spent dating.

Internal and external events force people to change.
People are separated by their jobs.
Sometimes they are unable to find and keep relationships
Money pressures affect most relationships.

We can nurture a relationship for years.
A single incident can determine its future in a day.
Despite this, many people care more about themselves than they do their relationships.
They remain ignorant of their lover's feelings.
The result is devastating.

These people are not good romantic partners.
They do not contribute to the relationship.
They do not know the meaning of love.

INTELLIGENCE:

Getting to know another person and getting known by them is a matter of controlling information.

The Art of War: Using Spies

[18]You need a creative leader and a worthy commander.
You must move your troops to the right places to beat others.
You must accomplish your attack and escape unharmed.
This requires foreknowledge.
You can obtain foreknowledge.
You can't get it from demons or spirits.
You can't see it from professional experience.
You can't check it with analysis.
You can only get it from other people.
You must always know the enemy's situation.

You must use five types of spies. **2**
You need local spies.
You need inside spies.
You need double agents.
You need doomed spies.
You need surviving spies.

[7]You need all five types of spies.
No one must discover your methods.
You will then be able to put together a true picture.
This is the commander's most valuable resource.

NETWORKS:

The key to gathering useful information is to have a range of different types of sources in your network.

[11]You need local spies.
Get them by hiring people from the countryside.

[13]You need inside spies.
Win them by subverting government officials.

The Art of Love: **Knowing Another**

We want to be creative lovers and valuable friends.
We must move our relationship in the right direction.
We must win commitment and be satisfied.
This requires communication.
You can get advanced warning.
You won't get it from astrology.
You won't get it from friends and family.
You can't reason this information out.
You can only get it by asking questions.
You must know your prospective partner's world.

2 We need to know five types of information.
We must know how our lover lives.
We must know their personalities.
We must know about their relationships.
We must know about their values.
We must know about their plans for the future.

We need all five types of information.
No one should feel that we are interrogating them.
We can put together a true picture of our sweetheart.
Communication is our most valuable resource.

We must know how our lover lives.
Learn this by getting to see where their home.

We must know about their personality.
We get this information from their friends and family.

> **INDIVIDUALS:**
> *We need to build personal relationships not only with our beloved but with the ones that our beloved loves.*

The Art of War: **Using Spies**

¹⁵You need double agents.
Discover enemy agents and convert them.

¹⁷You need doomed spies.
Deceive professionals into being captured.
Let them know your orders.
They then take those orders to your enemy.

²¹You need surviving spies.
Someone must return with a report.

Your job is to build a complete army. 3
No relations are as intimate as the ones with spies.
No rewards are too generous for spies.
No work is as secret as that of spies.

⁵If you aren't clever and wise, you can't use spies.
If you aren't fair and just, you can't use spies.
If you can't see the small subtleties, you won't get the truth from spies.

⁸Pay attention to small, trifling details!
Spies are helpful in every area.

¹⁰Spies are the first to hear information, so they must not spread information.
Spies who give your location or talk to others must be killed along with those to whom they have talked.

The Art of Love: **Knowing Another**

We must know about their relationships.
Get it by winning over friends and getting them to talk.

We must know our lover's values.
Share values by talking about politics and religion.
Let him or her know your beliefs.
Your lover will then respond to you.

We must know their dreams for the future.
We must sit down and discuss each other's plans.

3 Our job is to develop a solid relationship.
Nothing is as intimate as honest communication.
Nothing is as rewarding as knowing someone well.
Nothing is as sacred as a lover's trust.

We must be bright and perceptive to communicate well.
We must be open and unbiased to hear what is said.
If we aren't sensitive to subtleties, we won't hear the truth in what our lover is saying.

We must pay close attention to small details.
Communication is helpful in every area.

Intimate channels of communication demand that we keep information private.
The intimacy of any relationship is doomed if we cannot keep confidences secret.

The Art of War: Using Spies

4 You may want to attack an army's position.
You may want to attack a certain fortification.
You may want to kill people in a certain place.
You must first know the guarding general.
You must know his left and right flanks.
You must know his hierarchy.
You must know the way in.
You must know where different people are stationed.
You must demand this information from your spies.

¹⁰You want to know the enemy spies in order to convert them into your men.
You find a source of information and bribe them.
You must bring them in with you.
You must obtain them as double agents and use them as your emissaries.

¹⁴Do this correctly and carefully.
You can contact both local and inside spies and obtain their support.
Do this correctly and carefully.
You create doomed spies by deceiving professionals.
You can use them to give false information.
Do this correctly and carefully.
You must have surviving spies capable of bringing you information at the right time.

SPECIFICS:

The more specific your targets become, the more specific the information needed to win them.

The Art of Love: **Knowing Another**

4 We may want to advance our relationship.
We may have difficulties with our sweetheart.
We may have difficulties with family or friends.
We must first know our lover's opinion.
We must know our lover's defenses and insecurities.
We must know our lover's priorities.
We must know how to bring up a subject.
We must know what the sensitive topics are.
We get this information from communication.

We must want to get closer to our lover's family and friends to win them over.
We must be willing to spend time with them.
We must win them over.
We must get them to want the relationship and use them as go-betweens.

To do this correctly, we must be careful.
We need to have the support of co-workers, roommates, friends, and family.
To do this well, we must be sensitive.
We create "missionaries" by changing the perceptions of key people.
We must both be honest.
To do this correctly, we must be responsive.
We need to know that how well our plans for the future fit together.

> **INSIDERS:**
>
> *Our goal is to get inside the information loop so that we are in on the secrets that people keep the most private.*

The Art of War: Using Spies

²¹These are the five different types of intelligence work.
You must be certain to master them all.
You must be certain to create double agents.
You cannot afford to be too cost conscious in creating these double agents.

This technique created the success of ancient Shang. 5
This is how the Shang held its dynasty.

³You must always be careful of your success.
Learn from Lu Ya of Shang.

⁵Be a smart commander and a good general.
You do this by using your best and brightest people for spying.
This is how you achieve the greatest success.
This is how you meet the necessities of war.
The whole army's position and ability to move depends on these spies.

SOURCES:

Strategy is the science of leveraging information sources.

The Art of Love: **Knowing Another**

There are five different areas of communication.
We must be certain to master them all.
We must have friends supporting our relationship.
We cannot worry about how much time and effort it takes to develop mutual friends.

5 This is how people have been successful in romance.
This is how they build their relationships.

You must always be careful with your future.
Learn from successful relationships.

You must be a wise lover and a good friend.
You must put your best and efforts into knowing your intended.
This is how you create emotional bonds.
This is how you satisfy your lover.
Intimacy and the ability to get closer depend on good communication.

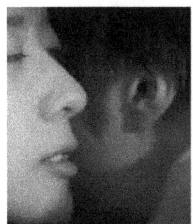

SUCCESS:

Success is based only caring to have superior knowledge.

Related Articles from *Sun Tzu's Playbook*

In his final chapter, Sun Tzu explains how to use information channels. To learn the step-by-step techniques involved, we recommend the Sun Tzu's Art of War Playbook *articles listed below.*

2.0.0 Developing Perspective: adding depth to competitive analysis.

2.1 Information Value: knowledge and communication as the basis of strategy.

2.1.1 Information Limits: making good decisions with limited information.

2.1.3 Strategic Deception: misinformation and disinformation in competition.

2.1.4 Surprise: how the creation of surprise depends on the nature of information.

2.2 Information Gathering: gathering competitive information.

2.2.1 Personal Relationships: why information depends on personal relationships.

2.2.3 Standard Terminology: how mental models must be shared to enable communication.

2.3 Personal Interactions: making progress through personal interactions.

2.3.4 Using Questions: using questions in gathering information and predicting reactions.

2.3.5 Infinite Loops: predicting reactions on the basis of the "you-know-that-I-know-that-you-know" problem.

2.3.6 Promises and Threats: the use of promises and threats as strategic moves.

2.4 Contact Networks: the range of contacts needed to create perspective.

2.4.1 Ground Perspective: getting information on a new competitive arena.

2.4.2 Climate Perspective: getting perspective on temporary external conditions.

2.4.3 Command Perspective: developing sources for understanding decision-makers.

2.4.4 Methods Perspective: developing contacts who understand best practices.

2.4.5 Mission Perspective: how we develop and use a perspective on motivation.

2.5 The Big Picture: building big-picture strategic awareness.

2.6 Knowledge Leverage: getting competitive value out of knowledge.

2.7 Information Secrecy: defining the role of secrecy in relationships.

Glossary of Key Strategic Concepts

This glossary is keyed to the most common English words used in the translation of *The Art of War*. Those terms only capture the strategic concepts generally. Though translated as English nouns, verbs, adverbs, or adjectives, the Chinese characters on which they are based are totally conceptual, not parts of speech. For example, the character for CONFLICT is translated as the noun "conflict," as the verb "fight," and as the adjective "disputed." Ancient written Chinese was a conceptual language, not a spoken one. More like mathematical terms, these concepts are primarily defined by the strict structure of their relationships with other concepts. The Chinese names shown in parentheses with the characters are primarily based on Pinyin, but we occasionally use Cantonese terms to make each term unique.

ADVANCE (JEUN 進): to move into new GROUND; to expand your POSITION; to move forward in a campaign; the opposite of FLEE.

ADVANTAGE, *benefit* (LI 利): an opportunity arising from having a better POSITION relative to an ENEMY; an opening left by an ENEMY; a STRENGTH that matches against an ENEMY'S WEAKNESS; where fullness meets emptiness; a desirable characteristic of a strategic POSITION.

AIM, *vision, foresee* (JIAN 見): FOCUS on a specific ADVANTAGE, opening, or opportunity; predicting movements of an ENEMY; a skill of a LEADER in observing CLIMATE.

ANALYSIS, *plan* (GAI 計): a comparison of relative POSITION; the examination of the five factors that define a strategic POSITION; a combination of KNOWLEDGE and VISION; the ability to see through DECEPTION.

ARMY: see WAR.

ATTACK, *invade* (GONG 攻): a movement to new GROUND; advancing a strategic POSITION; action against an ENEMY in the sense of moving into his GROUND; opposite of DEFEND; does not necessarily mean CONFLICT.

BAD, *ruined* (PI 圮): a condition of the GROUND that makes ADVANCE difficult; destroyed; terrain that is broken and difficult to traverse; one of the nine situations or types of terrain.

BARRICADED: see OBSTACLES.

BATTLE (ZHAN 戰): to challenge; to engage an ENEMY; generically, to meet a challenge; to choose a confrontation with an ENEMY at a specific time and place; to focus all your resources on a task; to establish superiority in a POSITION; to challenge an ENEMY to increase CHAOS; that which is CONTROLLED by SURPRISE; one of the four forms of ATTACK; the response to a DESPERATE SITUATION; character meaning was originally "big meeting," though later took on the meaning "big weapon"; not necessarily CONFLICT.

BRAVERY, *courage* (YONG 勇): the ability to face difficult choices; the character quality that deals with the changes of CLIMATE; courage of conviction; willingness to act on vision; one of the six characteristics of a leader.

BREAK, *broken, divided* (PO 破): to DIVIDE what is COMPLETE; the absence of a UNITING PHILOSOPHY; the opposite of UNITY.

CALCULATE, *count* (SHU 數): mathematical comparison of quantities and qualities; a measurement of DISTANCE or troop size.

CHANGE, *transform* (BIAN 變): transition from one CONDITION to another; the ability to adapt to different situations; a natural characteristic of CLIMATE.

CHAOS, *disorder* (JUAN 亂): CONDITIONS that cannot be FORESEEN; the natural state of confusion arising from BATTLE; one of six weaknesses of an organization; the opposite of CONTROL.

CLAIM, *position, form* (XING 形): to use the GROUND; a shape or specific condition of GROUND; the GROUND that you CONTROL; to use the benefits of the GROUND; the formations of troops; one of the four key skills in making progress.

CLIMATE, *heaven* (TIAN 天): the passage of time; the realm of uncontrollable CHANGE; divine providence; the weather; trends that CHANGE over time; generally, the future; what one must AIM at in the future; one of five key factors in ANALYSIS; the opposite of GROUND.

COMMAND (LING 令): to order or the act of ordering subordinates; the decisions of a LEADER; the creation of METHODS.

COMPETITION: see WAR.

COMPLETE: see UNITY.

CONDITION: see GROUND.

CONFINED, *surround* (WEI 圍): to encircle; a SITUATION or STAGE in which your options are limited; the proper tactic for dealing with an ENEMY that is ten times smaller; to seal off a smaller ENEMY; the characteristic of a STAGE in which a larger FORCE can be attacked by a smaller one; one of nine SITUATIONS or STAGES.

CONFLICT, *fight* (ZHENG 争): to contend; to dispute; direct confrontation of arms with an ENEMY; highly desirable GROUND that creates disputes; one of nine types of GROUND, terrain, or stages.

CONSTRICTED, *narrow* (AI 狹): a confined space or niche; one of six field positions; the limited extreme of the dimension distance; the opposite of SPREAD-OUT.

CONTROL, *govern* (CHI 治): to manage situations; to overcome disorder; the opposite of CHAOS.

DANGEROUS: see SERIOUS.

DANGERS, *adverse* (AK 阨): a condition that makes it difficult to ADVANCE; one of three dimensions used to evaluate advantages; the dimension with the extreme field POSITIONS of ENTANGLING and SUPPORTING.

DEATH, *desperate* (SI 死): to end or the end of life or efforts; an extreme situation in which the only option is BATTLE; one of nine STAGES or types of TERRAIN; one of five types of SPIES; opposite of SURVIVE.

DECEPTION, *bluffing, illusion* (GUI 詭): to control perceptions; to control information; to mislead an ENEMY; an attack on an opponent's AIM; the characteristic of war that confuses perceptions.

DEFEND (SHOU 守): to guard or to hold a GROUND; to remain in a POSITION; the opposite of **ATTACK**.

DETOUR (YU 迂): the indirect or unsuspected path to a POSITION; the more difficult path to ADVANTAGE; the route that is not DIRECT.

DIRECT, *straight* (JIK 直): a straight or obvious path to a goal; opposite of DETOUR.

DISTANCE, *distant* (YUAN 遠): the space separating GROUND; to be remote from the current location; to occupy POSITIONS that are not close to one another; one of six field positions; one of the three dimensions for evaluating opportunities; the emptiness of space.

DIVIDE, *separate* (FEN 分): to break apart a larger force; to separate from a larger group; the opposite of JOIN and FOCUS.

DOUBLE AGENT, *reverse* (FAN 反): to turn around in direction; to change a situation; to switch a person's allegiance; one of five types of spies.

EASY, *light* (QING 輕): to require little effort; a SITUATION that requires little effort; one of nine STAGES or types of terrain; opposite of SERIOUS.

EMOTION, *feeling* (XIN 心): an unthinking reaction to AIM, a necessary element to inspire MOVES; a component of esprit de corps; never a sufficient cause for ATTACK.

ENEMY, *competitor* (DIK 敵): one who makes the same CLAIM; one with a similar GOAL; one with whom comparisons of capabilities are made.

ENTANGLING, *hanging* (GUA 懸): a POSITION that cannot be returned to; any CONDITION that leaves no easy place to go; one of six field positions.

EVADE, *avoid* (BI 避): the tactic used by small competitors when facing large opponents.

FALL APART, *collapse* (BENG 崩): to fail to execute good decisions; to fail to use a CONSTRICTED POSITION; one of six weaknesses of an organization.

FALL DOWN, *sink* (HAAM 陷): to fail to make good decisions; to MOVE from a SUPPORTING POSITION; one of six weaknesses of organizations.

FEELINGS, *affection, love* (CHING 情): the bonds of relationship; the result of a shared PHILOSOPHY; requires management.

FIGHT, *struggle* (DOU 鬥): to engage in CONFLICT; to face difficulties.

FIRE (HUO 火): an environmental weapon; a universal analogy for all weapons.

FLEE, *retreat, northward* (BEI 北): to abandon a POSITION; to surrender GROUND; one of six weaknesses of an ARMY; opposite of ADVANCE.

FOCUS, *concentrate* (ZHUAN 專): to bring resources together at a given time; to UNITE forces for a purpose; an attribute of having a shared PHILOSOPHY; the opposite of *divide*.

FORCE (LEI 力): power in the simplest sense; a GROUP of people bound by UNITY and FOCUS; the relative balance of STRENGTH in opposition to WEAKNESS.

FORESEE: see AIM.

FULLNESS: see STRENGTH.

GENERAL: see LEADER.

GOAL: see PHILOSOPHY.

GROUND, *situation, stage* (DI 地): the earth; a specific place; a specific condition; the place one competes; the prize of competition; one of five key factors in competitive analysis; the opposite of CLIMATE.

GROUPS, *troops* (DUI 隊): a number of people united under a shared PHILOSOPHY; human resources of an organization; one of the five targets of fire attacks.

INSIDE, *internal* (NEI 內): within a TERRITORY or organization; an insider; one of five types of spies; opposite of OUTSIDE.

INTERSECTING, *highway* (QU 衢): a SITUATION or GROUND that allows you to JOIN; one of nine types of terrain.

JOIN (HAP 合): to unite; to make allies; to create a larger FORCE; opposite of DIVIDE.

KNOWLEDGE, *listening* (ZHI 知): to have information; the result of listening; the first step in advancing a POSITION; the basis of strategy.

LAX, *loosen* (SHII 弛): too easygoing; lacking discipline; one of six weaknesses of an army.

LEADER, *general, commander* (JIANG 將): the decision-maker in a competitive unit; one who LISTENS and AIMS; one who manages TROOPS; superior of officers and men; one of the five key factors in analysis; the conceptual opposite of SYSTEM, the established methods, which do not require decisions.

LEARN, *compare* (XIAO 效): to evaluate the relative qualities of ENEMIES.

LISTEN, *obey* (TING 聽): to gather KNOWLEDGE; part of ANALYSIS.

LISTENING: see KNOWLEDGE.

LOCAL, *countryside* (XIANG 鄉): the nearby GROUND; to have KNOWLEDGE of a specific GROUND; one of five types of SPIES.

MARSH (ZE 澤): GROUND where footing is unstable; one of the four types of GROUND; analogy for uncertain situations.

METHOD: see SYSTEM.

MISSION: see PHILOSOPHY.

MOMENTUM, *influence* (SHI 勢): the FORCE created by SURPRISE set up by STANDARDS; used with TIMING.

MOUNTAINS, *hill, peak* (SHAN 山): uneven GROUND; one of four types of GROUND; an analogy for all unequal SITUATIONS.

MOVE, *march, act* (HANG 行): action toward a position or goal.

NATION (GUO 國): the state; the productive part of an organization; the seat of political power; the entity that controls an ARMY or competitive part of the organization.

OBSTACLES, *barricaded* (XIAN 險): to have barriers; one of the three characteristics of the GROUND; one of six field positions; as a field position, opposite of UNOBSTRUCTED.

OPEN, *meeting, crossing* (JIAO 交): to share the same GROUND without conflict; to come together; a SITUATION that encourages a race; one of nine TERRAINS or STAGES.

OPPORTUNITY: see ADVANTAGE.

OUTMANEUVER (SOU 走): to go astray; to be FORCED into a WEAK POSITION; one of six weaknesses of an army.

OUTSIDE, *external* (WAI 外): not within a TERRITORY or ARMY; one who has a different perspective; one who offers an objective view; opposite of INTERNAL.

PHILOSOPHY, *mission, goals* (TAO 道): the shared GOALS that UNITE an ARMY; a system of thought; a shared viewpoint; literally "the way"; a way to work together; one of the five key factors in ANALYSIS.

PLATEAU (LIU 陸): a type of GROUND without defects; an analogy for any equal, solid, and certain SITUATION; the best place for competition; one of the four types of GROUND.

RESOURCES, *provisions* (LIANG 糧): necessary supplies, most commonly food; one of the five targets of fire attacks.

RESTRAINT: see TIMING.

REWARD, *treasure, money* (BAO 賞): profit; wealth; the necessary compensation for competition; a necessary ingredient for

VICTORY; VICTORY must pay.

SCATTER, *dissipating* (SAN 散): to disperse; to lose UNITY; the pursuit of separate GOALS as opposed to a central MISSION; a situation that causes a FORCE to scatter; one of nine conditions or types of terrain.

SERIOUS, *heavy* (CHONG 重): any task requiring effort and skill; a SITUATION where resources are running low when you are deeply committed to a campaign or heavily invested in a project; a situation where opposition within an organization mounts; one of nine STAGES or types of TERRAIN.

SIEGE (GONG CHENG 攻城): to move against entrenched positions; any movement against an ENEMY'S STRENGTH; literally "strike city"; one of the four forms of attack; the least desirable form of attack.

SITUATION: see GROUND.

SPEED, *hurry* (SAI 馳): to MOVE over GROUND quickly; the ability to ADVANCE POSITIONS in a minimum of time; needed to take advantage of a window of opportunity.

SPREAD-OUT, *wide* (GUANG 廣): a surplus of DISTANCE; one of the six GROUND POSITIONS; opposite of CONSTRICTED.

SPY, *conduit, go-between* (GAAN 間): a source of information; a channel of communication; literally, an "opening between."

STAGE: see GROUND.

STANDARD, *proper, correct* (JANG 正): the expected behavior; the standard approach; proven methods; the opposite of SURPRISE; together with SURPRISE creates MOMENTUM.

STOREHOUSE, *house* (KU 庫): a place where resources are stockpiled; one of the five targets for fire attacks.

STORES, *accumulate, savings* (JI 糧): resources that have been stored; any type of inventory; one of the five targets of fire attacks.

STRENGTH, *fullness, satisfaction* (SAT 壹): wealth or abundance or resources; the state of being crowded; the opposite of XU, empty.

SUPPLY WAGONS, *transport* (ZI 輜): the movement of RESOURCES through DISTANCE; one of the five targets of fire attacks.

SUPPORT, *supporting* (ZHII 支): to prop up; to enhance; a GROUND POSITION that you cannot leave without losing STRENGTH; one of six field positions; the opposite extreme of ENTANGLING.

SURPRISE, *unusual, strange* (QI 奇): the unexpected; the innovative; the opposite of STANDARD; together with STANDARDS creates MOMENTUM.

SURROUND: see CONFINED.

SURVIVE, *live, birth* (SHAANG 生): the state of being created, started, or beginning; the state of living or surviving; a temporary condition of fullness; one of five types of spies; the opposite of DEATH.

SYSTEM, *method* (FA 法): a set of procedures; a group of techniques; steps to accomplish a GOAL; one of the five key factors in analysis; the realm of groups who must follow procedures; the opposite of the LEADER.

TERRITORY, *terrain*: see GROUND.

TIMING, *restraint* (JIE 節): to withhold action until the proper time; to release tension; a companion concept to MOMENTUM.

TROOPS: see GROUPS.

UNITY, *whole, oneness* (YI 一): the characteristic of a GROUP that shares a PHILOSOPHY; the lowest number; a GROUP that acts as a unit; the opposite of DIVIDED.

UNOBSTRUCTED, *expert* (TONG 通): without obstacles or barriers; GROUND that allows easy movement; open to new ideas; one of six field positions; opposite of OBSTRUCTED.

VICTORY, *win, winning* (SING 勝): success in an endeavor; getting a reward; serving your mission; an event that produces more than it consumes; to make a profit.

WAR, *competition, army* (BING 兵): a dynamic situation in which POSITIONS can be won or lost; a contest in which a REWARD can be won; the conditions under which the rules of strategy work.

WATER, *river* (SHUI 水): a fast-changing GROUND; fluid CONDITIONS; one of four types of GROUND; an analogy for change.

WEAKNESS, *emptiness, need* (XU 處): the absence of people or resources; devoid of FORCE; the point of ATTACK for an ADVANTAGE; a characteristic of GROUND that enables SPEED; poor; the opposite of STRENGTH.

WIN, *winning*: see VICTORY.

WIND, *fashion, custom* (FENG 風): the pressure of environmental forces.

Index of Topics in *The Art of War*

This index identifies significant topics, keyed to the chapters, block numbers (big numbers in text), and line numbers (tiny numbers). The format is chapter:block.lines.

Advantage adapting for 8:1.14
 calculating 1:5
 fighting for 7:2.1-17
 four types of terrain 9:1.25
 guided by 7.1.9-13
 winning 11:2.8
Adversity, using 11:4.15
Analysis see Planning
Army misuse of 2:1.16-22
 moving w/o supplies 7:2.18
 nation's support of 3:4.1-4
 overturn by killing general 8:5.11
 politicians' control of 3:4.12-17
 preserving 10:3.17-21
 six weaknesses 10:2
  disorganized 10:2:21-25
  fall apart 10:2.17-20
  fall down 10:2.15-16
  outmaneuvered 10:2.10-12
  retreat 10:2:26-30
  too lax 10:2:13-14
 size 2:1.12-15
Attack defense, and 6:2.1-8
 fire attacks 12:1; 12:3
 five situations 12:2
 on cities 3:2.5-16
 types and priority 3:2.1
 when to attack 4:2; 12:4
Battle chaos of 5:4.1-6
 effortless battles 4:3.17
 good battles 4:3.12-16
 picking 1:5; 4:1.6-8; 6:3.10-17
 provoking 10:3.10-16
 secrecy of time and place 6:5.1-12
 small 3:3.1-7
 timing and momentum 5:2.7-8
 winning and losing 3:6
Chaos 5:4
Climate definition of 1:1.19-22
 seasonal changes 9:3.1-15
Commander
 characteristics of 1:1.28
 five faults 8:5
 foolish and wise 3:1.12-15
 good and bad 1:2.12-19
 killing 8:5.11
 obtaining foreknowledge 13:1.18-27
 ordering men 11:3.29
 problems adapting 8:1.16-21
 profession of 11:5
 spoiling men 10:4.5-9
 using opportunities to attack 12:4
 using spies 13:3.5-7; 13:5.5-9
Commitment 3:3.8-9
Communication 7:4
Conflict advantage in 7:1.14
 avoiding disasters in 7:1.5
 rules for 7:6.4-13
Costs distance, effect of 2:3.1-2

 minimizing 2:2.3-8; 2:4
 war 13:1.1-9
Deception as essence of war 1:4
 in movement 7:3.1
Defense attack, and 6:2.1-8
 when to defend 4:2
Dividing enemies 6:4
 plunder 7:3.10
Emptiness and Fullness
 battlefield 6:1.1-2
 four forms of 6:7.1-8
 movement, using in 6:2.1-8
Enemy adjusting to 6:5.7-12; 6:8.8-11; 7:6.1
 changing the condition of 6.1.9-11
 controlling 6.1.5-11; 8:3.1-3
 creates opportunity 4:1.1-5
 dividing 11:2.1-7
 feeding off of 2:4
 judging behavior 9:4.1-6; 9:5
 knowledge of 3:6
 large 5:1; 6:6.17-18
 not trusting 8:4.1-5
 predicting 10:3.3
 preparing for 11:2.10-19
 strength and weakness 6:5.13-16
Field Position
 six types 10:1
  barricaded 10:1.39-44
  constricted 10:1.33-38
  entangling 10:1.14-23
  spread out 10:1.45-48
  supporting 10:1.24-32
  unobstructed 10:1.7-13
Five Elements
 definition of 1:1.6-33
 importance of 1:1.34-37
 questions regarding 1:2.3-10
Foreseeing obtaining foreknowledge 13:1.18-27
 success and defeat 1:5
 soldiers' behavior 10:5.1
General see Commander
Ground calculating victory: 4:4.10-14
 definition 1:1.23-27
 four types 9:1
  marshes 9:1.15-20
  mountains 9:1.1-5
  plateaus 9:1.21-24
  water 9:1.6-14, 9:3
 high ground 9:2
 nine terrains (situations) 11:1
  bad 11:1.27-31
  confined 11:1.32-35
  controlling them 11:1.39-47, 11:6.16-24
  dangerous 11:1.24-26
  deadly 11:1.36-38
  disputed 11:1.15-17
  easy 11:1.13-14
  intersecting 11.1.21-23

218 *The Art of War Plus The Art of Love*

Knowledge
    open 11:1.18-20
    scattering 11:1.11-12
    enemy and self 3:6; 10:5.14-16
    environmental sources 9:4.7-23
    factors in war 11:7.7
    keys to success 3:5
    movement 7:2.21
    needed for attack 13:4.1-9
    time and place of battle 6:6.1-3
    trifling details 13:3.8
    when ignorance 11:7.1-6

Leader, Leadership see Commander

Methods
    calculating victory 4:4:4-16
    creativity 5:2.11-12
    definition 1:1.30-33
    getting information 13:2.7-8
    spies, using 13:4
    surprise and direct action 5:2.24-26

Momentum
    comparison to water 5:3.1-2
    crossbow analogy 5:3.10
    deception, use of 7:3.1
    good battles, creating 5:5
    people, using 5:5.5-12
    surprise, using 5:2.20-26

Movement
    based on knowledge 11:7.3-6
    inability to move 4:3.1-3
    knowledge, need for 7:2.21-28
    not into people 6:1.3-4
    using openings 6:3.6-9

Nation   supporting 3:4.1-4

Opportunity
    awaiting 4:1
    seeing not controlling 4:1.9

People
    battle, using in 4:5
    children analogy 10:4.1-4
    commitment 11:3.14-18
    communication, uniting for 7:4.6-11
    controlling 11:6.25-28
    esprit de corps 11:3.6-7
    morale 7:5.1-2; 7:5.10-12
    ordering men 11:3.29
    spoiling men 10:4.5-9

Philosophy
    defense 4:1.3
    definition 1:1.14-18
    invader 11:3.1; 11:6.1
    momentum, source of 5:5.5-12

Planning
    chaos, control of 5:4.10-11
    creativity in 8:2.1
    outside opinion 1:3.3
    questions, use of 1:2.1-17

Politics
    bureaucrats 13:1.12-17
    government, controlling 11:7.10; 11:8.1-5
    problems with 3:4

Position
    battles, winning with 4:3.17-20
    enemies, controlling with 5:4.16-23
    people, using to win 4:5
    strength and weakness 5:4.14-15
    taking 6:4; 6:7.5-15
    water analogy 6:8.1-11

Power   7:5.13-16

Problems
    as opportunities 7:1.6-8
    recovering from 11:7.30-31

Secrecy
    battle's time and place 6:5.1-12; 6:6.4-11
    hidden dangers 9:3.16-22
    movement 6:3.1-5
    planning 1:4.17-18
    spies 13:3.10-11

Size (of force)
    army 2:1.12
    controlling balance of 6:6.12
    different sizes, tactics for 3:3.12-18
    relative advantages of 3:3.19-20
    same methods 5:1

Soldiers see People

Speed
    haste and long wars 2:1.23-24
    hurrying, dangers of 7:2.4-12
    long delays 2:1.13

Spies
    five types 13:2; 13:4.10-21
    doomed 13:2.17-20
    double agents 13:2.15-16, 13:4.10-13
    inside 13:2.13-14
    local 13:2.11-12
    surviving 13:2.21-22
    work of 13:3.1

Surprise
    infinite nature of 5:2.4-6
    sources of 5:2.11-20
    surprise and direct action 5:2.24
    winning with 5:2

Terrain see Ground

Time
    changes over 6:8.12-15, 13:1.10-11
    energy levels 7:5.3-9
    fire attacks 12:1.9-16
    recover over 5:2.7
    seasonal changes 9:3.1-15
    timing 5:3.4.11

Unity
    focus on openings 6:4
    value of 3:1.1-12

Victory
    assuring 4:3.24
    field position, use of 10:3.1
    five keys to 3:5
    letting it happen 6:6.15-16
    making it easy 4:3.4-20
    making it pay 2:5
    opportunity for 4:1.1-5

War
    balance in winning 4:4.15-16
    commitment to 3:3.8-9
    dangers and benefits 2:2.1-2
    destruction by 2:3.8-15
    effective 3:3.1-2
    expensive 2:1.1-11; 2:5.1-2; 13:1.1-5
    long 2:1.23-26
    messiness of 5:4.4
    nature of 1:1.1-5; 1:4.1-2
    rules for 3:3.12-18
    start of 11:8.12-15

Weakness and Strength
    adapting to 8:2.2
    position from 5:4.14-15
    too weak to fight 9:6

Weather see Climate

Winning see Victory

Index of Topics in The Art of War   **219**

About the Author

Gary Gagliardi

This book's award-winning translator and primary author, Gary Gagliardi, is America's leading authority on Sun Tzu's *The Art of War*. A frequent guest on radio and television talk shows, Gary has written over wenty books on strategy. Ten of his books on Sun Tzu's methods have won award recognition in business, self-help, career, sports, philosophy, multicultural, and youth nonfiction categories.

Gary began studying Sun Tzu's philosophy over thirty years ago. His understanding of strategy was proven in the business world, where his software company became one of the Inc. 500 fastest-growing companies in America and won numerous business awards. After selling his software company, Gary began writing about and teaching Sun Tzu's strategic philosophy full time.

He has spoken all over the world on a variety of topics concerning competition, from modern technology to ancient history. His books have been translated into many languages, including Japanese, Thai, Korean, Russian, Indonesian, and Spanish.

Today he splits his time between Seattle and Las Vegas, living with his wife, Rebecca, and travels extensively for speaking engagements all over the world.

garyg@suntzus.com

@strategygary

Want to learn more about Sun Tzu's strategy?

SUNTZUS.COM
SCIENCE OF STRATEGY INSTITUTE

eBooks
Audio books
Audio seminars
Online training

Art of War and Strategy Books By Gary Gagliardi

Sun Tzu's Art of War Rule Book in Nine Volumes
Sun Tzu's The Art of War Plus The Art of Sales: Strategy for the Sales Warrior
9 Formulas for Business Success: the Science of Strategy
The Golden Key to Strategy: Everyday Strategy for Everyone
The Art of War Plus The Chinese Revealed
The Art of War Plus The Art of Management: Straegy for Management Warriors
Art of War for Warrior Marketing: Strategy for Conquering Markets
The Art of War Plus The Art of Politics: Strategy for Campaigns (with Shawn Frost)
Making Money By Speaking: The Spokesperson Strategy
The Warrior Class: 306 Lessons in Strategy
The Art of War for the Business Warrior: Strategy for Entrepreneurs
The Art of War Plus The Warrior's Apprentice: Strategy for Teens
The Art of War Plus Strategy for Sales Managers: Strategy for Sales Groups
The Ancient Bing-fa: Martial Arts Strategy
Strategy Against Terror: Ancient Wisdom for Today's War
The Art of War Plus The Art of Career Building: Strategy for Promotion
Sun Tzu's Art of War Plus Parenting Teens
The Art of War Plus Its Amazing Secrets: The Keys to Ancient Chinese Science
Art of War Plus Art of Love: Strategy for Romance

www.ingramcontent.com/pod-product-compliance
Lightning Source LLC
Chambersburg PA
CBHW060340170426
43202CB00014B/2831